Literature

and the Language Arts

Understanding Literature

**UNIT NINE
RESOURCE**

THE EMC MASTERPIECE SERIES

EMCParadigm Publishing Saint Paul, Minnesota

Staff Credits

Editorial

Laurie Skiba
Editor

Brenda Owens
Associate Editor

Lori Ann Coleman
Associate Editor

Diana Moen
Associate Editor

Gia Marie Garbinsky
Assistant Editor

Jennifer Joline Anderson
Assistant Editor

Janice Johnson
Curriculum Specialist

Paul Spencer
Art and Photo Researcher

Chris Bohen
Editorial Assistant

Katherine S. Link
Editorial Assistant

Marie Couillard
Editorial Consultant

Design

Shelley Clubb
Production Manager

C. Vern Johnson
Senior Designer

Parkwood Composition
Compositor

Cover Credits

Cover Designer: C. Vern Johnson

The Human Condition, 1934. Rene Magritte.

The Farm, 1921–1922. Joan Miró.

The Persistence of Memory, 1931. Salvador Dali.

ISBN 0-8219-2156-8
© 2001 EMC Corporation

Published by EMC/Paradigm Publishing
875 Montreal Way
St. Paul, Minnesota 55102
800-328-1452
www.emcp.com
E-mail: educate@emcp.com

Printed in the United States of America.
10 9 8 7 6 5 4 3 2 1 XXX 00 01 02 03 04 05 06 07 08 09

Contents

Selection Worksheet 9.1

"Simple Song," page 711

READER RESPONSE ACTIVITIES

Graphic Organizer, page 711

Summarize the central idea from each stanza to help you find the theme(s) in the poem. Use the graphic organizer below.

stanza 1	
stanza 2	
stanza 3	

Reader's Journal, page 711

How would you respond to someone who is similar to you? to someone who is different from you?

_____

_____

_____

_____

Guided Reading Questions

PAGE 712

What do we say when we are moving toward someone?

_____

_____

What do we say when we are leaving someone?

_____

_____

Respond to the Selection, page 712

Do you have any friends with whom it is "easy to be together"? What makes them so easy to get along with? Do you have any friends who are very different from you? How do you get along with them?

_____

_____

_____

_____

INVESTIGATE, INQUIRE, AND IMAGINE, PAGE 713

Recall

1a. When two people move toward each other, what are they thinking and feeling? What are they thinking and feeling as they end their relationship?

_____

_____

_____

_____

2a. In the third stanza, what words does the speaker use to describe each of us?

_____

_____

_____

_____

3a. What is love not able to outlive?

_____

_____

_____

_____

Interpret

1b. What does it mean to say "your thoughts are my brothers"? Should this line be taken literally or figuratively? When is it easy for people to be together, and when is it difficult?

_____

_____

_____

_____

2b. What do these words suggest about people's ability to relate to one another?

_____

_____

_____

_____

3b. What does it mean to have an open hand and an open eye? What does the speaker mean by "the door in the chest standing open"? Should this be taken literally or figuratively?

_____

_____

_____

_____

Analyze

4a. Identify the relationship between the first stanza and the second stanza. What changes take place from stanza 1 to stanza 2? What does each stanza represent? What does the speaker mean when he or she says, in stanza 3, "We are not different nor alike"? What does the speaker say we are instead?

_____

_____

_____

_____

_____

Synthesize

4b. In your own words, summarize the first and second stanzas. What is the speaker saying about what brings people together and what pushes them apart? How does stanza 3 serve as a response to stanzas 1 and 2?

_____

_____

_____

_____

Perspective

5a. Do you agree or disagree with the speaker that "loving is an act / that cannot outlive / the open hand / the open eye / the door in the chest standing open" (lines 14–18)? Explain. Do you agree or disagree with the speaker that people are neither different nor alike? If you agree, what do you think we are instead? If you disagree, what makes us different? What makes us alike?

_____

_____

_____

_____

_____

Empathy

5b. What could you conclude about the speaker's experience with love based on lines 14–18? What advice is the speaker giving about relationships?

_____

_____

_____

_____

_____

UNDERSTANDING LITERATURE, PAGE 713

SPEAKER AND FIRST-PERSON POINT OF VIEW. Who do you think is the speaker of this poem? Whom is the speaker referring to when he or she uses the word *we*? How might the poem be different if the speaker had used *I* instead of *we*?

_____

_____

_____

_____

THEME. Refer to the chart you completed for the Graphic Organizer. Identify one major theme that runs through this poem.

_____

WRITER'S JOURNAL, PAGE 714

1. Write a **statement of belief** about one of the following: friendship, diversity, or interpersonal communication.

   _____

   _____

   _____

   _____

   _____

   _____

   _____

   _____

   _____

   _____

   _____

2. Create an **image** for an abstract noun such as *peace, justice, love, hate,* and so on.

   _____

   _____

   _____

   _____

   _____

   _____

   _____

   _____

   _____

   _____

   _____

3. Write a **poem** about how it feels to begin a new relationship with someone or how it feels to separate from a relationship.

_____

_____

_____

_____

_____

_____

_____

_____

_____

_____

Selection Check Test 4.9.1

"Simple Song"

CHECKING YOUR READING

Short Answer

1. In your opinion, what does Piercy mean by "When we are going toward someone"?

_____

2. How do we perceive the person "we are going toward," according to Piercy?

_____

3. How do we perceive the person we are leaving, according to Piercy?

_____

4. Are either of those perceptions correct, according to the last stanza?

_____

5. What do you think lines 14–18 mean?

_____

_____

LITERARY TOOLS

Matching

Write the letter of the correct answer in the blank provided.

_____ 1. a central idea in a literary work

_____ 2. the character who narrates a poem

_____ 3. uses words such as *he, she,* and *it*

_____ 4. uses words such as *I* and *we*

    a. speaker

    b. first-person point of view

    c. third-person point of view

    d. theme

Selection Test 4.9.2

"Simple Song"

INSIGHTFUL READING

True or False

_____ 1. We think the person we are going toward is just like us.

_____ 2. It is easy to communicate when we are leaving someone.

_____ 3. We cannot agree with the person we are leaving.

_____ 4. We are really alike.

_____ 5. Love cannot outlive our search for something new.

UNDERSTANDING LITERARY CONCEPTS

Short Answer

1. From what point of view is the poem presented? How do you know?

   _____

   _____

2. How does the use of point of view affect your reading of the poem?

   _____

   _____

3. How does Piercy build up to the theme that love cannot outlive the need for newness and excitement?

   _____

   _____

CRITICAL WRITING

Essay

Choose <u>one</u> of the following prompts and write an essay. Complete <u>both</u> the Prepare to Write and Write sections of the prompt you choose. Use your own paper as necessary.

1. Stanzas

PREPARE TO WRITE. Reread "Simple Song," and consider the division of the poem into stanzas. Why has Piercy divided the poem in such a way? Does each stanza contain a separate idea? Does the content of each stanza build on the content of the previous stanza?

_____

_____

_____

_____

WRITE. In an essay, analyze the division of the poem and the author's use of stanzas as they relate to content. Use quotations from the poem to support your opinions.

_____

_____

_____

_____

_____

_____

_____

_____

_____

_____

_____

_____

_____

_____

_____

_____

_____

_____

2. Do You Agree?

PREPARE TO WRITE. Consider each stanza of the poem as you decide whether you agree with the ideas included. Do you think the poem captures a universal attitude? Do you think one stanza does, but not the others?

_____

_____

_____

_____

_____

WRITE. Write a personal response to the poem, explaining whether you agree with the ideas presented.

_____

_____

_____

_____

_____

_____

_____

_____

_____

_____

_____

_____

_____

_____

_____

_____

_____

_____

_____

_____

Selection Worksheet 9.2

"Prayer to the Pacific," page 715

READER RESPONSE ACTIVITIES

Graphic Organizer, page 715

As you read, complete the cluster chart below listing what you learn about the sea turtles. One example has been done for you.

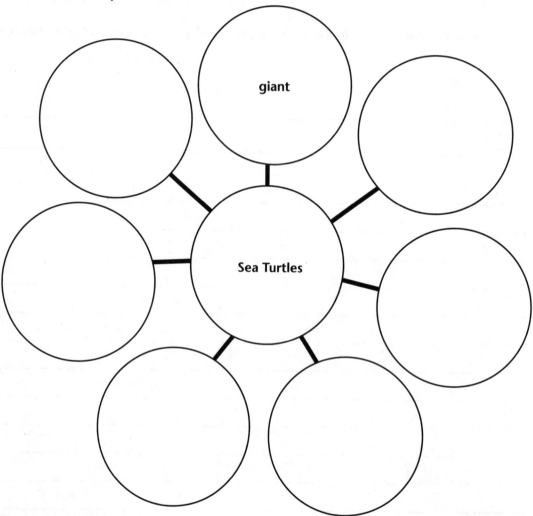

Reader's Journal, page 715

What story can you tell about the ocean?

_____

_____

_____

_____

Guided Reading Questions

PAGE 716

To where did the speaker travel?

_____

_____

What does the speaker carry back?

_____

_____

Respond to the Selection, page 717

What gift of nature does the speaker relate that finds its source in the myth of the sea turtles?

_____

_____

_____

_____

INVESTIGATE, INQUIRE, AND IMAGINE, PAGE 718

Recall

1a. Where does the speaker live?

_____

_____

2a. What does the speaker take from the ocean?

_____

_____

_____

Interpret

1b. Why does the speaker mention where she is from?

_____

_____

2b. Why does the speaker intend "to suck and to taste" the stones?

_____

_____

_____

Analyze

3a. What evidence can you find that demonstrates the speaker's understanding and feelings toward her culture?

_____

_____

_____

Synthesize

3b. How does the speaker appreciate nature, intellectually or physically? Give evidence to support your answer.

_____

_____

_____

Perspective

4a. Is the speaker's reaction to the ocean under-
standable?

_____

_____

_____

_____

Empathy

4b. If you were the speaker, what would you
remember about the ocean once you went
back to the "southwest land of sandrock"?

_____

_____

_____

_____

_____

UNDERSTANDING LITERATURE, PAGE 718

SIMILE. To what is the largeness of the ocean compared in the first stanza? What is the purpose of this
simile?

_____

_____

MYTH. Review the cluster chart you completed for the Graphic Organizer. What event does the myth in
stanza 3 attempt to explain? What modern explanation might science give to explain this migration?

_____

_____

WRITER'S JOURNAL, PAGE 719

1. Imagine you are the speaker and have returned home. Write a **journal entry** expressing what your
trip to the ocean meant to you.

_____

_____

_____

_____

_____

_____

_____

_____

_____

2. Write **interview questions** to ask the speaker about her beliefs.

_____

_____

_____

_____

_____

_____

_____

_____

_____

_____

3. Write a **myth** that explains the migration of Native Americans to America in a different way from that of the sea turtles.

_____

_____

_____

_____

_____

_____

_____

_____

_____

INTEGRATING THE LANGUAGE ARTS, PAGE 719

Language, Grammar, and Style

RECOGNIZING CLAUSES AND PHRASES. Read the Language Arts Survey 3.81, "Groups of Words That Function as One Part of Speech," and 3.82, "Phrases." Then identify the underlined parts of the following sentences as clauses (C) or phrases (P).

1. When the speaker left her "southwest land of sandrock," she went to the ocean. _____

2. She looked at the "pale water" with discerning eyes. _____

3. To her way of thinking, the ocean was as big as "the myth of origin." _____

4. The Indians who came east to America rode across the ocean on giant sea turtles. _____

5. If you hold out your tongue, you too can swallow raindrops "clear from China." _____

Media Literacy

TYING ORAL TRADITION TO FICTION. In the introduction to one of Silko's works, LaVonne Ruoff states, "Silko emphasizes the need to return to rituals and oral traditions of the past in order to rediscover the basis for one's cultural identity." Read about Silko's writings on the Internet and make a list of her writings for which this statement proves true. You might find it useful to access the University of Minnesota's "Voices From the Gaps: Women Writers of Color" Internet site at http://voices.cla.umn.edu/authors/ LeslieMarmonSilko.html. Use the research log below to record your findings and to note the sources you consulted in your research.

Research Log

Research Findings on Silko's Writings:

_____

_____

_____

_____

_____

_____

_____

_____

_____

Sources Used:

_____

_____

_____

_____

Selection Check Test 4.9.3

"Prayer to the Pacific"

CHECKING YOUR READING

Short Answer

1. Where does the speaker travel?

_____

_____

2. What does the speaker return to the Earth?

_____

_____

3. What do the round stones symbolize for the speaker?

_____

_____

4. What do lines 6–10 describe?

_____

_____

5. According to lines 17–19, how did the Indians reach the Americas?

_____

_____

LITERARY TOOLS

Short Answer

1. What is a simile?

_____

_____

2. What is a myth?

_____

_____

3. Which myth does Silko mention in line 5?

_____

_____

Selection Test 4.9.4

"Prayer to the Pacific"

INSIGHTFUL READING

True or False

_____ 1. The speaker returns four stones to the ocean.

_____ 2. Rain clouds drift from the west.

_____ 3. The Indians came from Europe.

Short Answer

1. How does the speaker describe her home?

_____

_____

2. Which ocean is the speaker visiting? How do you know?

_____

_____

_____

UNDERSTANDING LITERARY CONCEPTS

Short Answer

1. What is the implication of the simile "the moving blue water / Big as the myth of origin"?

_____

_____

2. What two phenomena are explained in the myth?

_____

_____

3. Is there a mythological character presented in the poem? If so, who?

_____

_____

_____

CRITICAL WRITING

Essay

Choose <u>one</u> of the following prompts and write an essay. Complete <u>both</u> the Prepare to Write and Write sections of the prompt you choose. Use your own paper as necessary.

1. Analyzing Literary Techniques in the Poem

PREPARE TO WRITE. Leslie Marmon Silko uses a number of techniques to make "Prayer to the Pacific" a successful poem. Take notes on those techniques and examples of them in the poem as you prepare to write your essay. You may want to consider such techniques as personification, imagery, and simile. You might also explore the way Silko has shaped the poem on the page. What does the poem with its line breaks look like? How is it a concrete poem?

_____

_____

_____

_____

_____

_____

WRITE. Write an essay that analyzes the techniques Silko uses to make "Prayer to the Pacific" an effective poem.

_____

_____

_____

_____

_____

_____

_____

_____

_____

_____

_____

_____

_____

_____

2. Exploring Myth

PREPARE TO WRITE. This poem incorporates the myth of sea turtles carrying the first peoples to a new land across the Pacific Ocean. Many native stories connect turtles to the creation and growth of the world. How does this poem make this connection? Why do you think turtles are so important to native cultures? What characteristics of turtles make them an important part of such myths?

_____

_____

_____

_____

_____

_____

_____

_____

_____

WRITE. Write an essay that synthesizes your thoughts and understanding of the role turtles play in native myths and in "Prayer to the Pacific."

_____

_____

_____

_____

_____

_____

_____

_____

_____

_____

_____

_____

_____

_____

_____

_____

Selection Worksheet 9.3

"The Cabuliwallah," page 720

READER RESPONSE ACTIVITIES

Graphic Organizer, page 720

Fill in the chart below listing facts you learn about the Cabuliwallah and the technique of characterization that they demonstrate. One example has been done for you.

Facts about Cabuliwallah	Technique
Wore the loose, soiled clothing of his people and a tall turban; carried a bag on his back and boxes of grapes in his hand.	direct description

Reader's Journal, page 720

Describe a friendship you have had with an adult. What topics did you talk about?

_____

_____

_____

_____

Guided Reading Questions

PAGE 721

What does Mini do all the time? How do her parents feel about this tendency?

_____

_____

Why is Mini frightened of the Cabuliwallah?

_____

_____

PAGE 722

What does the narrator do when he sees his daughter with the Cabuliwallah's gifts? What does the Cabuliwallah do in return?

_____

_____

How does the Cabuliwallah overcome Mini's fears?

_____

_____

PAGE 723

What is the double meaning of the words "father-in-law's house"?

_____

_____

What are Mini's mother's feelings about the Cabuliwallah?

_____

_____

PAGE 724

Why is Rahmun arrested?

_____

_____

PAGE 725

How does the situation change the joke the Cabuliwallah and Mini had shared?

_____

_____

Who appears on the night of Mini's wedding? In what ways has he changed? How does the narrator recognize him?

_____

_____

How does Mini's father feel about Rahmun's arrival?

_____

_____

PAGE 726

What has Rahmun carried with him all these years? How does this change Mini's father's feelings?

_____

_____

What new meaning does Mini and Rahmun's old joke have?

_____

_____

_____

What happens as a result of Mini's father giving money to Rahmun? What effect does Mini's father think it has on the festivities?

_____

_____

Respond to the Selection, page 726

Was the Cabuliwallah's imprisonment just or unjust?

_____

_____

_____

_____

_____

INVESTIGATE, INQUIRE, AND IMAGINE, PAGE 727

Recall

1a. What can Mini, the narrator's five-year-old daughter, not live without doing?

_____

_____

_____

2a. What is Mini's first reaction to the Cabuliwallah?

_____

_____

_____

Interpret

1b. What troubles the narrator when Mini is silent?

_____

_____

_____

2b. What actions on the part of Mini and the Cabuliwallah show that they enjoy one another's friendship?

_____

_____

_____

3a. What gift does Rahmun bring to Mini on her wedding day?

_____

_____

_____

3b. What actions on the part of Mini show that she has grown up?

_____

_____

_____

Analyze

4a. Analyze the relationship between Rahmun and Mini. What things do they do with each other? How do they feel toward one another? Back up your answers with examples from the text.

_____

_____

_____

_____

_____

Synthesize

4b. Based on the relationship between Rahmun and Mini you described in question 4a, predict what their relationship would have been like if Rahmun had never gone to jail. In what ways would Rahmun's life be different if they never separated? In what ways would Mini's life be different?

_____

_____

_____

_____

_____

Evaluate

5a. What is the reason Rahmun develops a special friendship with young Mini? Do you think this is a good reason? Why, or why not?

_____

_____

_____

_____

Extend

5b. Why do you think the narrator reacts the way he does when Rahmun shows him the impression of his daughter's hand on the piece of paper? How do you think the narrator's reaction would have been different if he, himself, were not a father of a daughter?

_____

_____

_____

_____

UNDERSTANDING LITERATURE, PAGE 727

THEME. What underlying theme is highlighted by the change in Mini, as seen by Rahmun, at the end of the story?

_____

_____

_____

CHARACTERIZATION. Review the chart you completed for the Graphic Organizer. What techniques does Tagore use to characterize Rahmun? Which of Rahmun's behaviors show that he dearly loves his only daughter?

_____

_____

_____

_____

WRITER'S JOURNAL, PAGE 728

1. Pretend you are Rahmun. Write a **letter** to your daughter in the mountains of Afghanistan, telling her how you feel about her, what you keep always in your possession, and why you have been separated.

_____

_____

_____

_____

_____

_____

_____

_____

_____

_____

_____

2. Write a **wedding invitation** for Rahmun.

_____

_____

_____

_____

_____

_____

_____

_____

_____

_____

_____

3. Imagine Rahmun returns to see the narrator after he has seen his daughter. Write a **dialogue** between the two men in which they discuss what their daughters were like when they were little and the relationship they have with them now that they are grown. Did Rahmun's daughter forgive him after his long absence? Did Mini forgive her father after he pared down her wedding celebration?

_____

_____

_____

_____

_____

_____

_____

_____

_____

_____

_____

INTEGRATING THE LANGUAGE ARTS, PAGE 728

Language, Grammar, and Style

USING THE ACTIVE VOICE. Read the Language Arts Survey 3.37, "Making Passive Sentences Active." Determine whether each of the following sentences is written in the passive or the active voice. Rewrite those that are in the passive voice, using the active voice instead. Write *OK* if a sentence needs no correction.

1. A hero and a heroine were created by the narrator for his story.

_____

2. Ruhman was called the Cabuliwallah by the people of Calcutta.

_____

3. Ruhman accepted the money for the almonds and raisins that the narrator handed him.

_____

4. He was taken to jail by the police for hitting a customer.

_____

5. Ruhman was released from his jailers on the day of Mini's wedding.

_____

Vocabulary

Using Context Clues to Estimate Word Meaning. Read the following passages from "The Cabuliwallah" and use context clues to estimate the meaning of the underlined word.

EXAMPLE

The Cabuliwallah had overcome the child's first terror by a <u>judicious</u> bribery of nuts and almonds, and the two were now great friends.

<u>judicious: well thought out</u>

1. Entering at this moment, I saved her from <u>impending</u> disaster and proceeded to make my own inquiries.

   <u>impending</u>: _____

2. But she would not show it, and with instant <u>composure</u> replied: "Are you going there?"

   <u>composure</u>: _____

3. "It is a <u>euphemism</u> for jail, the place where we are well cared for at no expense."

   <u>euphemism</u>: _____

4. "Ah," he would say, shaking his fist at an invisible policeman, "I will thrash my father-in-law!" Hearing this, and picturing the poor, uncomfortable relative, Mini would go into peals of laughter, joined by her <u>formidable</u> friend.

   <u>formidable</u>: _____

5. I could see the string of camels bearing merchandise, and the company of turbaned merchants carrying queer old firearms and some of their spears down toward the plains. I could see—but at this point Mini's mother would intervene, <u>imploring</u> me to "beware of that man."

   <u>implore</u>: _____

Selection Check Test 4.9.5

"The Cabuliwallah"

CHECKING YOUR READING

Short Answer

1. How old is Mini when she meets the Cabuliwallah?

   _____

2. How does Mini react to the Cabuliwallah at first?

   _____

3. How does their relationship change in the following weeks?

   _____

4. What happens to the Cabuliwallah as he is trying to collect his debts?

   _____

5. How does Mini react to the Cabuliwallah when he returns on her wedding day?

   _____

VOCABULARY IN CONTEXT

Sentence Completion

Fill in each blank below with the most appropriate word from Words for Everyday Use from "The Cabuliwallah." You may not use every word, and you may need to change the tense of some words.

precarious   impending   judicious   composure   formidable   implore   pervade

1. She faced the _____ task of cleaning the long-neglected attic.

2. The tragic hero faced _____ doom.

3. The jurors must make a(n) _____ decision concerning the guilt of the defendant.

4. Even in the face of danger, the woman kept her _____.

5. The smell of garbage _____ the neighborhood next to the landfill.

LITERARY TOOLS

Short Answer

1. What is the definition of *theme?*

   _____

   _____

2. What is characterization?

   _____

   _____

3. What are the three major techniques of characterization?

   _____

   _____

Selection Test 4.9.6

"The Cabuliwallah"

INSIGHTFUL READING

True or False

_____ 1. Mini talks constantly as a child.

_____ 2. Mini's father is a lawyer.

_____ 3. The Cabuliwallah wins Mini's affection by giving her nuts.

_____ 4. *Father-in-law's house* is a euphemism for *jail.*

_____ 5. The Cabuliwallah stays for Mini's wedding.

Matching

Write the letter of the correct answer in the blank provided.

_____ 1. is the hero of a novel

_____ 2. chatters constantly as a child

_____ 3. is a peddler from Afghanistan

_____ 4. is afraid of many things and is described as timid

_____ 5. enjoys Mini's chatter even when interrupted from his writing

    a. Mini

    b. Mini's father

    c. Mini's mother

    d. Cabuliwallah

    e. Pratap Singh

VOCABULARY IN CONTEXT

Sentence Completion

Fill in each blank below with the most appropriate word from Words for Everyday Use from "The Cabuliwallah." You may not use every word, and you may need to change the tense of some words.

euphemism   fettered   composure   precarious   pervade   implore

1. *Was let go* is a(n) ————————— for *fired.*

2. "Please, please, please come with me," she —————————.

3. He found himself in a(n) ————————— position when asked to choose whom he liked best.

4. The prisoner's hands were ————————— behind his back.

5. I could barely regain my ————————— after the embarrassing incident.

UNDERSTANDING LITERARY TECHNIQUES

Short Answer

1. Literary works often have numerous themes. What are two themes of this story?

_____

_____

2. What is the primary technique used to reveal the narrator's character?

_____

_____

3. What technique is not used to portray the Cabuliwallah and Mini?

_____

_____

CRITICAL WRITING

Essay

Write an essay, completing <u>both</u> the Prepare to Write and Write sections below. Use your own paper as necessary.

Father-Daughter Relationships

PREPARE TO WRITE. Consider the father-daughter relationship Tagore portrays in this story. Is the relationship typical? How so or how not? How does the relationship develop over time? Do you think it will change further over time? Explain.

_____

_____

_____

_____

WRITE. In an essay, analyze the father-daughter relationship Tagore presents. Be sure to support your opinion with examples from the text.

_____

_____

_____

_____

_____

_____

_____

_____

_____

_____

_____

_____

_____

_____

_____

_____

_____

_____

_____

Selection Worksheet 9.4

"New Dog," page 729

READER RESPONSE ACTIVITIES

Graphic Organizer, page 729

Complete the cluster chart to list statements from the poem that point to the speaker's emotion. One example has been done for you.

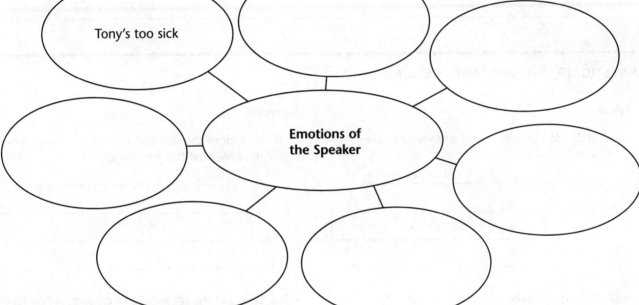

Tony's too sick

Emotions of the Speaker

Reader's Journal, page 729

What assumptions do you have about dying people?

_____

_____

_____

_____

Guided Reading Questions

PAGE 730

What does Wally want?

_____

_____

PAGE 731

How is Wally able to interact with the dog?

_____

_____

Respond to the Selection, page 731

What process has the speaker been witnessing?

_____

_____

_____

_____

INVESTIGATE, INQUIRE, AND IMAGINE, PAGE 732

Recall

1a. What do Jimi and Tony feel they can't keep? Why?

_____

_____

_____

_____

2a. Why does Wally want a new dog?

_____

_____

_____

_____

3a. What does the speaker wonder?

_____

_____

_____

_____

Interpret

1b. How does the situation of Jimi and Tony foreshadow what happens to Wally?

_____

_____

_____

_____

2b. Why can the speaker say that Beau is "perfect" for the dying Wally?

_____

_____

_____

_____

_____

3b. Does the speaker approve or disapprove of Wally's wanting a new dog?

_____

_____

_____

_____

Analyze

4a. About his poetic inspiration, Mark Doty says, "I wait to be haunted, as it were, by an image. What happens is something I see registers on a deeper level than most experience does. A seal in the harbor, or the wreck of a fishing boat. I'll feel this tug in my memory. Then I'll begin describing it to try to capture it. In the process of describing it I begin to understand what it is about the image that's compelling. It's not enough to describe it: the image is a vehicle for something I'm trying to understand." Identify the compelling image of Wally that informs this poem.

_____

_____

_____

_____

Synthesize

4b. What is Mark Doty trying to understand by writing this poem?

_____

_____

_____

_____

_____

Perspective

5a. Evaluate the role the speaker plays in Wally's life.

_____

_____

_____

_____

Empathy

5b. Compare and contrast the attitude toward death in Garrett Hongo's "The Legend" and Mark Doty's "New Dog."

_____

_____

_____

_____

UNDERSTANDING LITERATURE, PAGE 732

PARADOX. What is the paradox in this poem?

_____

_____

LYRIC POEM. Review the cluster chart you completed for the Graphic Organizer. What emotions of the speaker are implied in this lyric poem?

_____

_____

WRITER'S JOURNAL, PAGE 733

1. Imagine you are the speaker and Wally has died. Write a **eulogy** in which you remember your friend and his attitude toward life.

_____

_____

_____

_____

_____

_____

_____

_____

_____

_____

2. Imagine you are Wally. Write a **journal entry** in which you explain what your new dog, Beau, means to you.

_____

_____

_____

_____

_____

_____

_____

_____

_____

_____

3. Write a **paragraph** explaining whether or not Wally fits your image of a dying person.

_____

_____

_____

_____

_____

_____

_____

_____

_____

_____

_____

INTEGRATING THE LANGUAGE ARTS, PAGE 733

Language, Grammar, and Style

ADDING MODIFIERS. Read the Language Arts Survey 3.39, "Adding Colorful Language to Sentences." Then rewrite each of the following sentences, adding an appropriate adjective or adverb.

1. Tony is ill.

_____

2. The speaker is a friend of Wally.

_____

3. Beau is a dog.

_____

4. Wally touches the dog.

_____

5. Wally fights death.

_____

Study and Research

ON DEATH AND DYING. Research the stages of dying as described by Elisabeth Kübler-Ross. Use the research log below to record your findings and to note the sources you consulted in your research. Then, on your own paper, write a report identifying and describing each stage. Determine which stage you think Wally is in in "New Dog" and explain your assessment.

Research Log

Research Findings on Stages of Dying:

_____

_____

_____

_____

_____

_____

_____

_____

_____

_____

_____

_____

_____

_____

_____

_____

_____

_____

_____

_____

Sources Used:

_____

_____

_____

_____

_____

Selection Check Test 4.9.7

"New Dog"

CHECKING YOUR READING

Short Answer

1. What is wrong with Wally?

   _____

2. Why does the narrator go to Jimi and Tony's home?

   _____

3. What happens when he arrives?

   _____

4. Where does the speaker go after he leaves Jimi and Tony's home?

   _____

5. What does the speaker find there?

   _____

LITERARY TOOLS

Short Answer

1. What is a paradox?

   _____

2. What is a lyric poem?

   _____

3. What emotions does the speaker express in this poem?

   _____

Selection Test 4.9.8

"New Dog"

INSIGHTFUL READING

True or False

———— 1. Jimi and Tony give their dog to the speaker.

———— 2. Tony is too sick to care for the dog.

———— 3. Wally does not want a new dog.

———— 4. The speaker does not find a dog at the shelter.

———— 5. Beau is the perfect dog for Wally.

UNDERSTANDING LITERARY CONCEPTS

Short Answer

1. What paradoxical idea is presented in this poem?

_____

_____

2. How does the speaker express his emotions in this poem?

_____

_____

3. What, in your opinion, affects the speaker most?

_____

_____

CRITICAL WRITING

Essay

Choose <u>one</u> of the following prompts and write an essay. Complete <u>both</u> the Prepare to Write and Write sections of the prompt you choose. Use your own paper as necessary.

1. Beau's Effect

PREPARE TO WRITE. Reread the poem, and consider the effect that Beau has on the life of Wally, as well as on the life of the speaker. What has Beau's presence added to their lives?

_____

_____

_____

WRITE. In a few paragraphs, discuss what Beau has brought to the lives of the speaker and Wally. Use quotations from the poem to support your opinion.

_____

_____

_____

_____

_____

_____

_____

_____

_____

_____

_____

_____

_____

_____

_____

_____

_____

_____

_____

_____

2. Through Wally's Eyes

PREPARE TO WRITE. As you read the poem, consider what Wally might be thinking as each event occurs. How might he feel if the speaker were to return without a dog? Do you think he was excited at the prospect of taking Jimi and Tony's dog?

_____

_____

_____

_____

WRITE. Write a poem about the same events from Wally's point of view. Include his emotions and expectations about the new dog, as well as his feelings about his illness.

_____

_____

_____

_____

_____

_____

_____

_____

_____

_____

_____

_____

_____

_____

_____

_____

_____

_____

_____

Selection Worksheet 9.5

"1910," page 734

READER RESPONSE ACTIVITIES

Reader's Journal, page 734

Have you ever been wrongly accused of something or been judged unfairly because of race, sex, or ethnic background? Explain.

_____

_____

_____

_____

Guided Reading Questions

PAGE 735

With whom did Doña Luz walk in the evenings?

_____

_____

PAGE 736

What did Mr. Upton force Doña Luz to do?

_____

_____

Respond to the Selection, page 736

Do you think Mr. Upton deserved what happened to him? Why, or why not?

_____

_____

_____

_____

INVESTIGATE, INQUIRE, AND IMAGINE, PAGE 738

Recall

1a. Who was Doña Luz, and how was she regarded in her hometown in Mexico?

_____

_____

2a. What happens when Doña Luz goes into Upton's Five-and-Dime? What does Mr. Upton say to her?

_____

_____

_____

3a. Where does Doña Luz walk in the last five lines of the poem?

_____

_____

Analyze

4a. What details show you what kind of person Doña Luz is? Compare how Doña Luz was treated in her native town to how she was treated when she arrived in El Paso.

_____

_____

_____

_____

Evaluate

5a. Predict what Mr. Upton will do next. Do you think he will guess who is responsible for what happened to his store?

_____

_____

_____

_____

_____

Interpret

1b. How can you tell how Doña Luz was regarded by those in her home town?

_____

_____

2b. What does the encounter with Mr. Upton reveal about him?

_____

_____

_____

_____

3b. What do you think happened to Mr. Upton's store?

_____

_____

_____

_____

Synthesize

4b. What does this poem show about the attitudes some Americans held toward immigrants from Mexico? How did they judge the newcomers?

_____

_____

_____

_____

_____

Extend

5b. How is the experience of Doña Luz similar to that of the speaker in "Not Knowing, in Aztlán"? Which do you think is worse—to be judged harshly for "something you did" or because of "something you are"? Explain.

_____

_____

_____

_____

_____

UNDERSTANDING LITERATURE, PAGE 738

CHARACTERIZATION. What method or methods did the author of "1910" use to create the character of Doña Luz? Explain, giving examples. Do you get a complete picture of who this woman is, or just a glimpse?

_____

_____

_____

_____

IRONY AND IRONY OF SITUATION. What is ironic about the judgment Upton makes of Doña Luz? How might this be considered an example of irony of situation?

_____

_____

_____

_____

WRITER'S JOURNAL, PAGE 739

1. Imagine that Upton is being taken to court for discriminating against Mexican immigrants. Write the **opening statement** that might be delivered by the prosecuting attorney in this case.

_____

_____

_____

_____

_____

_____

_____

_____

_____

2. Imagine that you are Doña Luz. Write a **letter of complaint** addressed to Mr. Upton, protesting the way you were treated when you visited his store. Use correct business letter format, inventing the addresses for Doña Luz and for the store.

_____

_____

_____

_____

_____

_____

_____

_____

_____

3. Mr. Upton's policy of searching all Mexican customers is obviously unfair. Write a **store policy** for his Five-and-Dime that would instruct employees to treat all customers fairly. Include guidelines for how an employee should deal with an actual shoplifter.

_____

_____

_____

_____

_____

_____

_____

_____

_____

_____

_____

_____

INTEGRATING THE LANGUAGE ARTS, PAGE 739

Language, Grammar, and Style

PROPER NOUNS AND ADJECTIVES. Read the Language Arts Survey 3.95, "Proper Nouns and Adjectives." You will notice that in the poem "1910" *Mexico* is a proper noun and *Mexican* is a proper adjective. *Judge* is another proper noun in the poem. It normally should not be capitalized unless it is used with a name, as in "Judge Luz." Write down the other proper nouns you find in "1910."

_____

_____

_____

Form a proper noun and a proper adjective for each of the following common nouns.

EXAMPLE: Political party: Democrat (noun); Democratic (adjective)

1. state

_____   _____

2. country

_____   _____

3. scientist

_____   _____

4. literary movement

_____   _____

5. writer

_____   _____

Study and Research

MEXICAN HISTORY. Mexico has had not one revolutionary war, but two. Research the Mexican Revolution of 1810. How and where did the movement begin? Who were some of the heroes of the Revolution? How did the war finally end? Use the research log below to record your findings and to note the sources you consulted in your research. Then, on your own paper, write a report about your findings. Be sure to document your sources in a bibliography. For correct bibliographic format, see the Language Arts Survey 5.40, "Making Bibliographies and Bibliography Cards." As an alternative, you may wish to research the siege that took place during March–May 1867, which Mexicans commemorate as Cinco de Mayo, or you may choose to research the more recent uprising of Zapatista rebels based in Chiapas, a southern state of Mexico.

Research Log

Research Findings on Mexican Revolutionary History:

_____

_____

_____

_____

_____

_____

_____

_____

Sources Used:

_____

_____

_____

Selection Check Test 4.9.9
"1910"

CHECKING YOUR READING

Short Answer

1. How would you describe Doña Luz's character?

   _____

2. How does she react when she and her family must flee from Villa?

   _____

3. What event causes her to show a sign of weakness?

   _____

4. What do you think the black shawl and black gloves symbolize?

   _____

5. What happens to Upton's Five-and-Dime?

   _____

LITERARY TOOLS

Matching

Write the letter of the correct answer in the blank provided.

_____ 1. the difference between appearance and reality

_____ 2. the use of literary techniques to create a character

_____ 3. when an event occurs that violates the expectations of the characters, the reader, or the audience

    a. characterization

    b. irony

    c. irony of situation

Selection Test 4.9.10

"1910"

INSIGHTFUL READING

True or False

_____ 1. In Mexico, people bowed their heads when Doña Luz passed them.

_____ 2. Doña Luz wore a black shawl and gloves whenever she left home.

_____ 3. She cries about her fear of Villa.

_____ 4. Upton accuses Doña Luz of stealing from his store.

_____ 5. Upton's store prospers.

UNDERSTANDING LITERARY CONCEPTS

Short Answer

1. How would you describe Doña Luz's character?

_____

_____

2. What techniques does Mora use to characterize Doña Luz? Provide examples of each.

_____

_____

3. What is ironic about Upton accusing Doña Luz of stealing?

_____

_____

CRITICAL WRITING

Essay

Choose one of the following prompts and write an essay. Complete both the Prepare to Write and Write sections of the prompt you choose. Use your own paper as necessary.

1. Connecting Two Poems

PREPARE TO WRITE. Complete the Venn diagram below to compare and contrast the situation in Pat Mora's poem "1910" and the situation in Tino Villanueva's poem "Not Knowing, in Aztlán."

Situation in "1910"   **Situation in "Not Knowing, in Aztlán"**

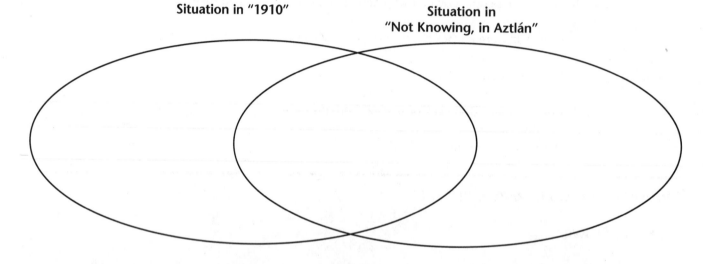

WRITE. Write a brief essay in which you compare and contrast the situations in "1910" and "Not Knowing, in Aztlán." Then explain which character—Doña Luz or the speaker in "Not Knowing, in Aztlán" is in a more powerful position, and why.

_____

_____

_____

_____

_____

_____

_____

_____

_____

_____

_____

_____

_____

2. Character Analysis

PREPARE TO WRITE. Reread the poem, and take notes on the character of Doña Luz. You might use a cluster diagram to organize your notes. What do you know about her from her actions? the descriptions of her?

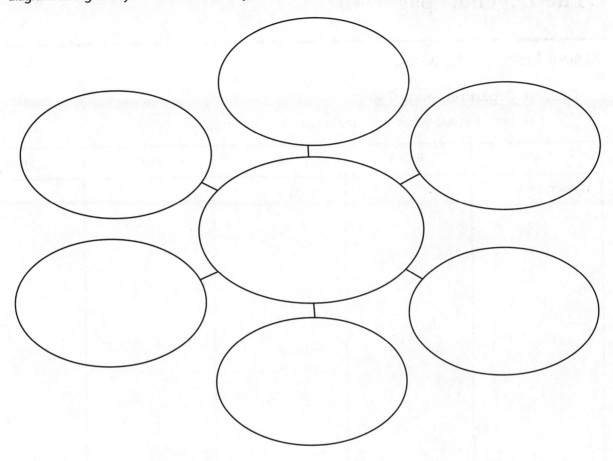

WRITE. In an essay, analyze the character of Doña Luz as portrayed by Mora. Be sure to support your opinions with details from the text.

_____

_____

_____

_____

_____

_____

_____

_____

_____

_____

_____

_____

Selection Worksheet 9.6
"The Legend," page 740

READER RESPONSE ACTIVITIES

Graphic Organizer, page 740

Complete the chart below listing the sensory details in the poem.

Sight	Sound	Touch	Taste	Smell
snowing softly		snowing softly		

Reader's Journal, page 740

How do you react when you hear about violent acts in the news?

_____

_____

_____

_____

Guided Reading Questions

PAGE 741

What did the man just do?

_____

_____

PAGE 742

What happens to the man?

_____

_____

Respond to the Selection, page 743

What emotion does the speaker probably feel about imagining the victim in the hands of the weaver girl after his death?

_____

_____

_____

_____

INVESTIGATE, INQUIRE, AND IMAGINE, PAGE 743

Recall

1a. How is the man described?

_____

_____

2a. What is the man's ethnic origin?

_____

_____

_____

3a. What do the suffering man's noises mean to the bystanders?

_____

_____

_____

Analyze

4a. Identify associations that come to mind from the title.

_____

_____

_____

Interpret

1b. What does the description of the man reveal about his frame of mind?

_____

_____

2b. Why does the speaker mention the man's ethnic origin?

_____

_____

_____

3b. What does the reaction of the bystanders reveal about them?

_____

_____

_____

Synthesize

4b. Why do you think the poem is entitled "The Legend"?

_____

_____

_____

© EMC

Evaluate

5a. Evaluate Hongo's attitude toward violence in contemporary society.

_____

_____

_____

_____

_____

Extend

5b. Robert Frost liked to distinguish between grievances (complaints) and griefs (sorrows). He even suggested that grievances, which are propagandistic, should be restricted to prose, "leaving poetry free to go its way in tears." In what way does "The Legend" "go its way in tears"?

_____

_____

_____

_____

_____

_____

UNDERSTANDING LITERATURE, PAGE 743

TONE. What is the tone of the first stanza? What phrases and words create this tone?

_____

_____

_____

SENSORY DETAILS. Review the chart you completed for the Graphic Organizer. Which sensory details do you think are factual, and which do you think are imagined by the poet?

_____

_____

_____

WRITER'S JOURNAL, PAGE 744

1. Imagine you are one of the bystanders who has witnessed the man's murder. Write a **news article** about what you have observed. Use your own paper as necessary.

_____

_____

_____

_____

_____

_____

_____

_____

2. Imagine you are the man doing his laundry. Write a **journal entry** describing how your day went and your plans for the evening. Use your own paper as necessary.

_____

_____

_____

_____

_____

_____

_____

3. Focus on a person or a scene that you can observe closely. Take notes on what you actually see and what you imagine about what you see. Then write a lyric **poem** about your experience. Use your own paper as necessary.

_____

_____

_____

_____

_____

_____

_____

_____

_____

_____

INTEGRATING THE LANGUAGE ARTS, PAGE 744

Language, Grammar, and Style

ADVERB CLAUSES. Read about adjective, adverb, and noun clauses in the Language Arts Survey 3.83, "Clauses within a Sentence." Then identify the type of clause in each of the following sentences.

1. An Asian man <u>who has just done his wash for the week</u> steps into the twilight of early evening.

_____

2. A triangle of orange lights his face <u>when the sunset blazes the storefronts</u>.

_____

3. He negotiates the ice <u>which is slick</u>.

_____

4. Another man shoots the Asian man <u>after exiting the corner package store</u>.

_____

5. <u>Whoever shot the man</u> should be punished, don't you think?

_____

Study and Research

INTERNMENT CAMPS. Research the internment of Japanese Americans during World War II. Topics to include in your research are causes for internment, the condition of the camps, the impact of internment on Japanese Americans, and restitution. Use the research log below to record your findings and to note the sources you consulted in your research. Then make an oral presentation of your findings. If you choose to do your research on the Internet, one site you will find useful is The Detroit News at http://detnews.com/menu/stories/13546.htm. To find more articles on the Internet, key in the words "Japanese Internment Camps."

Research Log

Research Findings on Japanese Internment Camps:

_____
_____
_____
_____
_____
_____
_____
_____
_____
_____
_____
_____
_____
_____
_____
_____
_____

Sources Used:

_____
_____
_____
_____
_____
_____

Selection Check Test 4.9.11

"The Legend"

CHECKING YOUR READING

Short Answer

1. What is the setting of the poem?

   _____

2. What has the man just finished?

   _____

3. What does the man look like?

   _____

   _____

4. What happens to the man as he is placing his laundry in his car?

   _____

   _____

5. How does the speaker feel about the wounded man?

   _____

   _____

   _____

LITERARY TOOLS

Short Answer

1. What is tone?

   _____

2. What tone does the poem take toward the shooting?

   _____

   _____

3. What are sensory details?

   _____

   _____

Selection Test 4.9.12

"The Legend"

INSIGHTFUL READING

True or False

_____ 1. The man has just finished his dinner.

_____ 2. The man is of Asian descent.

_____ 3. The events take place in winter.

_____ 4. The man is stabbed by a boy.

_____ 5. The speaker truly empathizes with the wounded man.

UNDERSTANDING LITERARY CONCEPTS

Short Answer

1. To what sense does the following quotation appeal: "as a last flash of sunset / blazes the storefronts"?

    _____

    _____

2. What is the tone of the second stanza?

    _____

    _____

3. What is the tone of the last stanza?

    _____

    _____

CRITICAL WRITING

Essay

Choose <u>one</u> of the following prompts and write an essay. Complete <u>both</u> the Prepare to Write and Write sections of the prompt you choose. Use your own paper as necessary.

1. Analyzing Images of Light

PREPARE TO WRITE. Garrett Hongo makes interesting use of light in "The Legend." Complete the cluster chart below, diagramming different images of light in the poem.

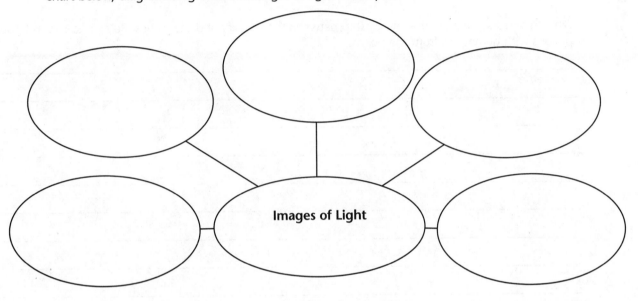

WRITE. Write an essay that analyzes the different ways the poem uses images of light, connecting the descriptions of light to what happens to the man who has finished his laundry.

_____

_____

_____

_____

_____

_____

_____

_____

_____

_____

_____

_____

2. The Speaker

PREPARE TO WRITE. Reread the poem, and consider the relationship the speaker feels toward the shooting victim. Do you think the speaker does not care about the victim? Do you think he cares more than he realizes?

_____

_____

_____

_____

WRITE. In an essay, analyze the relationship between the speaker and the victim. Be sure to support your opinions with quotations from the poem.

_____

_____

_____

_____

_____

_____

_____

_____

_____

_____

_____

_____

_____

_____

_____

_____

_____

_____

_____

_____

Selection Worksheet 9.7

"A White Woman of Color," page 745

READER RESPONSE ACTIVITIES

Graphic Organizer, page 745

Make a cluster chart listing the author's experiences and perceptions that inform her concept of race. One example has been done for you.

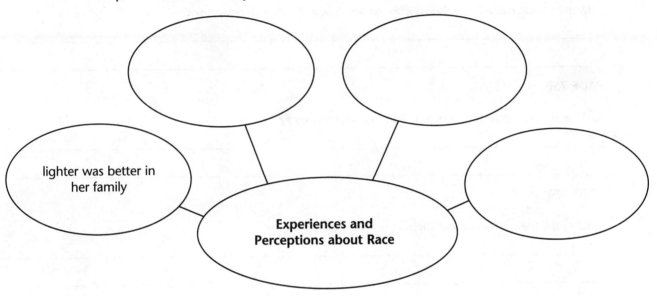

lighter was better in her family

Experiences and Perceptions about Race

Reader's Journal, page 745

Have you ever witnessed or personally experienced racism or discrimination? Describe your experience. How did it make you feel?

_____

_____

_____

_____

Guided Reading Questions

PAGE 746

Who was the "pride and joy" of the Álvarez family? What made her so special?

_____

_____

What differences did the mother and father have in regard to eating?

_____

_____

PAGE 748

As the saying goes, what do all Dominicans have behind their ears? What does the saying mean?

_____

_____

PAGE 749

What was the most important thing the maids did for the Álvarez children?

_____

_____

Despite being white Dominicans, what added "color" to their complexion?

_____

_____

PAGE 750

What things separated the author from her native culture?

_____

_____

PAGE 751

What did the author discover through reading books?

_____

_____

What aspects of the Álvarez family made their race struggle easier than that of other Dominicans living in the United States?

_____

_____

PAGE 752

How is the word "exclusive" ironic when used to define Latinos?

_____

_____

Respond to the Selection, page 752

How do you think you as an individual can help provide a positive multicultural model for a divided America?

_____

_____

_____

_____

INVESTIGATE, INQUIRE, AND IMAGINE, PAGE 753

Recall

1a. In what ways is the narrator's father "black"? In what ways is the narrator's mother "white"?

_____

_____

_____

_____

2a. Being a white Latina, how is the narrator a "colored" person?

_____

_____

_____

_____

3a. What did Maxine Hong Kingston, Toni Morrison, Gwendolyn Brooks, Langston Hughes, and other "colored" writers help the narrator realize?

_____

_____

_____

_____

Interpret

1b. Why do you think being black or having qualities that are "black" is looked down upon?

_____

_____

_____

_____

2b. What does the narrator mean by "culture color"?

_____

_____

_____

_____

3b. How did the narrator's life change after reading these authors' works?

_____

_____

_____

_____

Analyze

4a. Compare and contrast the racism experienced by the narrator in the Dominican Republic with the racism she experienced in the United States. How are they similar? How are they different?

_____

_____

_____

_____

Synthesize

4b. How would the author's life be different if she had never moved to the United States?

_____

_____

_____

_____

Perspective

5a. Álvarez says that in her writing she ultimately fights for "the reality that ethnicity and race are not fixed constructs or measurable quantities." Do you think she successfully conveys this message in the selection? Explain.

_____

_____

_____

_____

_____

Empathy

5b. What examples of diversity do you find in our culture?

_____

_____

_____

_____

_____

UNDERSTANDING LITERATURE

STYLE AND TONE. What are the style and tone of this essay?

_____

_____

_____

_____

PERSONAL ESSAY. Review the cluster chart you completed for the Graphic Organizer. Into what categories did you put the author's experiences and perceptions? What is an example for each category?

_____

_____

_____

_____

WRITER'S JOURNAL, PAGE 754

1. Write a **letter** to Julia Álvarez explaining how you reacted to her essay.

_____

_____

_____

_____

_____

_____

_____

_____

_____

_____

2. Write an **anecdote** of what it was like to grow up with your ethnicity.

_____

_____

_____

_____

_____

_____

_____

_____

_____

3. Write a **plan** for fighting racism that you can take as an individual or as a group.

_____

_____

_____

_____

_____

_____

_____

_____

_____

_____

_____

_____

INTEGRATING THE LANGUAGE ARTS, PAGE 754

Language, Grammar, and Style

SIMPLE TENSES. Read the Language Arts Survey 3.62, "Properties of Verbs: Tense." For each of the following sentences, circle the verbs and write which tense they are in.

1. The youngest Álvarez daughter resembled her mother's side of the family.

_____

2. In her essay, Álvarez maintains that ethnicity and race are not fixed constructs or measurable quantities.

_____

3. With other Latinos, the author will provide a positive multicultural, multiracial model to a divided America.

_____

4. The Dominican maids told Álvarez stories that had power over her when she was little.

_____

5. The author finds that writing connects her with Latino communities.

_____

Collaborative Learning & Study and Research

RESEARCHING A MOVEMENT. With several classmates, research one of the following movements: the Civil Rights Movement, the Women's Movement, or the Antiwar Movement (Vietnam). What led to the development of the movement? Who were the major figures in the movement? What changes occurred in American society because of the movement? How does the movement continue to affect us today? Refer to the Language Arts Survey 5.18–5.20, "Research Skills," to help you find the answers to these questions. Use the research log below to record your findings and to note the sources you consulted in your research. Then present your findings in an oral presentation.

Research Log

Research Findings on Movement:

_____

_____

_____

_____

_____

_____

_____

_____

_____

_____

Sources Used:

_____

_____

_____

_____

Vocabulary

USING BASE WORDS. Julia Álvarez describes her experiences after immigrating from the Dominican Republic to the United States in "A White Woman of Color." When different cultures come together they impact each other in significant ways, such as the borrowing of new vocabulary.

EXERCISE

Underline the root, or base word, of each word below and write the language from which it was borrowed. Then write a definition for the word. Use a dictionary if you don't know the root or the definition of a word.

EXAMPLE

<u>atroc</u>ity

<u>Latin; wicked or cruel act, object, or situation</u>

1. diaphanous

_____

2. aesthetic

_____

3. garish

_____

4. genocide

_____

5. paradigm

_____

6. patronage

_____

7. protocol

_____

8. relegated

_____

9. replenish

_____

10. solidarity

_____

Selection Check Test 4.9.13

"A White Woman of Color"

CHECKING YOUR READING

Short Answer

1. What does the author experience within her own family?

   _____

2. How does this experience manifest?

   _____

3. Describe Álvarez's mother.

   _____

4. Describe Álvarez's father.

   _____

5. What word has Álvarez learned to fear? Why?

   _____

VOCABULARY IN CONTEXT

Sentence Completion

Fill in each blank below with the most appropriate word from Words for Everyday Use from "A White Woman of Color." You may not use every word, and you may have to change the tense of some words.

　　emulate　　protocol　　elite　　entrepreneur　　relegated　　replenish　　solidarity

1. The teacher explained the _____ for the standardized test.

2. The restaurant caters to a(n) _____ crowd.

3. My classmate can _____ many famous actors.

4. At the end of the school year, the art instructor must _____ her supplies.

5. The boy who was afraid of the baseball was _____ to the right field position.

LITERARY TOOLS

Matching

Write the letter of the correct answer in the blank provided.

_____ 1. the emotional attitude toward the reader or toward the subject implied by a literary work

_____ 2. a short work of nonfictional prose on a single topic related to the life or interests of the writer

_____ 3. the manner in which something is said or written

      a. style

      b. tone

      c. personal essay

Selection Test 4.9.14

"A White Woman of Color"

INSIGHTFUL READING

True or False

_____ 1. In the author's family, lighter skin was considered more beautiful.

_____ 2. Álvarez's father was white.

_____ 3. Trujillo ordered the genocide of thousands of Haitians.

_____ 4. Álvarez was considered "a pretty white girl" because she stayed out of the sun.

_____ 5. The author and her family move to Jamaica Estates in New York.

Multiple Choice

Circle the letter of the correct answer.

1. Álvarez's oldest sister is ___.

    a. considered the most beautiful because of her coarse features

    b. considered the most beautiful because of her fine features

    c. considered the least beautiful because of her fine features

    d. considered the least beautiful because of her coarse features

2. The political power of the Dominican Republic ___.

    a. did not reside exclusively among the whites

    b. resided exclusively among the whites

    c. did not reside exclusively among the dark-skinned

    d. resided exclusively among the dark-skinned

3. Discrimination was not as prevalent in the Dominican Republic as in the United States because ___.

    a. the Dominicans embraced cultural diversity

    b. everyone's family had dark members

    c. the laws against discrimination were powerful

    d. fewer cultures reside in the Dominican Republic

4. During her time at the local school, when asked where she was from, the author immediately responded, ___.

   a. "The Dominican Republic"

   b. "None of your business"

   c. "Jamaica Estates"

   d. "Mexico"

5. When filling out the RACE question, the author believes the truest answer to be ___.

   a. OTHER

   b. BLACK

   c. HISPANIC

   d. CAUCASIAN

VOCABULARY IN CONTEXT

Sentence Completion

Fill in each blank below with the most appropriate word from Words for Everyday Use from "A White Woman of Color." You may not use every word, and you may have to change the tense of some words.

garish   cosmopolitan   aquiline   atrocity   aesthetic   proliferate   commodity

1. Being a _____, she favored upscale restaurants.

2. Her _____ outfit brought on the disapproval of her parents.

3. The mysterious murder of the young boy was a(n) _____ we would never forget.

4. The _____ structure of the vehicle was a popular selling point.

5. Knowledge is a priceless _____.

UNDERSTANDING LITERARY CONCEPTS

Short Answer

1. What do you think was Álvarez's aim in writing this personal essay?

   _____

2. What do you think is the tone of the essay?

   _____

3. How would you describe the style of the essay?

   _____

CRITICAL WRITING

Essay

Choose <u>one</u> of the following prompts and write an essay. Complete <u>both</u> the Prepare to Write and Write sections of the prompt you choose. Use your own paper as necessary.

1. Redefining Ethnicity

PREPARE TO WRITE. Julia Álvarez writes in "A White Woman of Color" that "What I came to understand and accept and ultimately fight for with my writing is the reality that ethnicity and race are not fixed constructs or measurable qualities." What does she mean by this statement? As you prepare to write your essay, take notes using the space below on how her essay reinforces her statement.

_____

_____

_____

_____

_____

_____

_____

_____

WRITE. In a brief essay, examine Álvarez's essay and chronicle ways in which she points out that "ethnicity and race are not fixed constructs or measurable qualities." Does her essay prove this statement? Explain, using evidence from the selection.

_____

_____

_____

_____

_____

_____

_____

_____

_____

_____

_____

_____

_____

2. The Multicultural, Multiracial Model

PREPARE TO WRITE. In the last sentence of the selection, Álvarez says, "Maybe as a group that embraces many races and differences, we Latinos can provide a positive multicultural, multiracial model to a divided America." Consider the ways America is divided and how those divisions could be helped by a positive model.

_____

_____

_____

_____

_____

_____

_____

_____

WRITE. In a brief essay, discuss the ethnic divisions in America as Álvarez encountered them, and as you yourself have experienced them. Then evaluate the ways in which Latinos might provide a positive multicultural, multiracial model to America.

_____

_____

_____

_____

_____

_____

_____

_____

_____

_____

_____

_____

_____

_____

_____

Selection Worksheet 9.8

"Something Could Happen to You," page 755

READER RESPONSE ACTIVITIES

Graphic Organizer, page 755

Use the cluster chart below to list the formative experiences the author has shortly after coming to the United States. One example has been done for you.

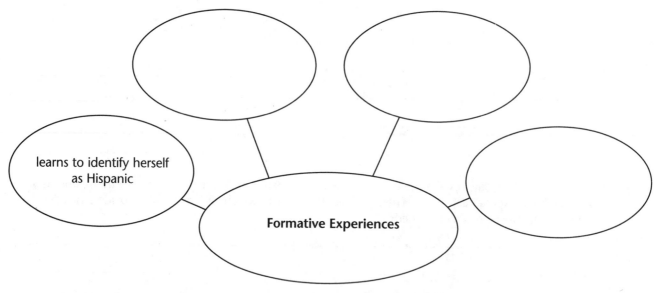

Reader's Journal, page 755

Have you ever visited a place different from the one where you live? Write a journal entry about what it felt like to be a newcomer in a strange place.

_____

_____

_____

_____

Guided Reading Questions

PAGE 756

Where did the author and her family come from?

_____

_____

PAGE 757

Why does Raymond walk with an "unbalanced gait"?

_____

_____

What is Tata's relation to the author?

_____

_____

What did the author see everywhere she looked in Brooklyn?

_____

_____

PAGE 758

Who is Tío Chico, and where does he sleep?

_____

_____

PAGE 759

Why was it hard for the author to enjoy the song on TV?

_____

_____

What class was the author put in, and why?

_____

_____

PAGE 760

What song did the author learn by heart?

_____

_____

Respond to the Selection, page 762

If you were the author, what would you find the most upsetting about your first few months in Brooklyn?

_____

_____

_____

_____

INVESTIGATE, INQUIRE, AND IMAGINE, PAGE 762

Recall

1a. Why do the author and her family come to the United States?

_____

_____

_____

2a. What does the author's mother caution her after learning she has gone outside to play?

_____

_____

_____

3a. What reaction did the author have toward her teacher's words?

_____

_____

_____

Interpret

1b. What does the United States offer that Puerto Rico does not?

_____

_____

_____

2b. What is the mother's attitude toward her new home? Why?

_____

_____

_____

3b. What does this tell you about the kind of attention she was getting in school?

_____

_____

_____

Analyze

4a. Analyze what the author learns about being Hispanic.

_____

_____

_____

_____

Synthesize

4b. Is the author proud of being Hispanic?

_____

_____

_____

_____

Evaluate

5a. What are the author's greatest obstacles as a recent immigrant?

_____

_____

_____

_____

_____

Extend

5b. Read the Related Reading. In what capacity does Negi serve when her mother loses her factory job? Compare Santiago's experience with Álvarez's.

_____

_____

_____

_____

_____

UNDERSTANDING LITERATURE, PAGE 762

DIALOGUE. What makes dialogue an effective way to show the author's newly acquired understanding of the term *Hispanic?* What do we learn about the author from this dialogue?

_____

_____

_____

_____

MEMOIR. Review the cluster chart you completed for the Graphic Organizer. How would you categorize the author's experiences that she recounts in this selection? Is her memoir autobiographical or biographical?

_____

_____

_____

WRITER'S JOURNAL, PAGE 763

1. Imagine you are thirteen-year-old Esmeralda. Write a **postcard** to a friend back in Puerto Rico telling him or her your perceptions of your new home and relating an interesting anecdote.

_____

_____

_____

_____

_____

_____

_____

_____

_____

2. Imagine you are Esmeralda's mother. Write a **letter** to your husband back in Puerto Rico explaining how the children are adapting to life in the United States. Express the fears and hopes you have for your children.

_____

_____

_____

_____

_____

_____

_____

_____

_____

3. About *Almost a Woman* Esmeralda Santiago has said, "When I began writing this book, I had no idea it would result in a dialogue about cultural identity." Write a **dialogue** between yourself and an imaginary teenager who is a young immigrant in your school. Discuss each of your cultural identities.

_____

_____

_____

_____

_____

_____

_____

_____

_____

_____

_____

_____

INTEGRATING THE LANGUAGE ARTS, PAGE 763

Language, Grammar, and Style

GERUNDS AND PARTICIPLES. Read the Language Arts Survey 3.80, "Verbals, Participles, Gerunds, and Infinitives." Then circle the gerunds and underline the present participles in the following sentences.

1. Esmeralda likes jumping rope with the neighbor girl.

2. On TV she watches the bouncing ball move from one word to the next.

3. Touching the building next door is easy because it is so close.

4. She began singing "The Star Spangled Banner" at school.

5. The drinking mug is for *café con leche.*

Study and Research

RESEARCHING IMMIGRATION. Research immigration to the United States today. Where do today's immigrants come from? How do they get here? Why did they leave their native country? Then research patterns of immigration one hundred years ago. Use the research log below to record your findings and to note the sources you consulted in your research. Then take a presentation to the class comparing immigration today with immigration one hundred years ago.

Research Log

Research Findings on Immigration:

_____

_____

_____

_____

_____

_____

_____

_____

_____

_____

_____

_____

_____

_____

_____

_____

_____

Sources Used:

_____

_____

_____

_____

_____

_____

Vocabulary

USING SUFFIXES. "Something Could Happen to You" describes the fear and confusion that immigrants to the United States have often experienced. Language and communication are crucial to survival and success.

EXERCISE

Complete each word in the left-hand column by adding one of the following suffixes. Then match the completed word with its definition in the right-hand column. Write the letter of the correct meaning next to the completed word.

–al   –ent   –ous   –an   –y   –ed   –ate

EXAMPLE

fastid<u>ous</u>   <u>b</u>

1. scrupul_____   a. damaged

2. lank_____   b. meticulous

3. vac_____   c. sturdy

4. pung_____   d. fascinated

5. sever_____   e. acrid

6. mesmeriz_____   f. cut

7. ephemer_____   g. temporary

8. marr_____   h. native of Cuba

9. substanti_____   i. tall

10. Cub_____   j. make free

Selection Check Test 4.9.15

"Something Could Happen to You"

CHECKING YOUR READING

Short Answer

1. What was the weather like when Santiago arrived in New York?

   _____

2. When Santiago first arrived, what was her impression of New York?

   _____

3. What does the neighbor girl tell Santiago?

   _____

4. How does Santiago feel about this revelation?

   _____

5. Why is Santiago placed in a class for students with behavior problems?

   _____

VOCABULARY IN CONTEXT

Sentence Completion

Fill in each blank below with the most appropriate word from Words for Everyday Use from "Something Could Happen to You." You may not use every word, and you may have to change the tense of some words.

severed   subtle   substantial   mesmerized   vacate   subdue   marred

1. She dropped _____ hints about what she wanted for her birthday.

2. When the fire alarm rang, we were forced to _____ the building.

3. The child was _____ by the light dancing off the crystal unicorn.

4. When he changed jobs, he _____ all ties with his former employer.

5. She was _____ by the bad news.

LITERARY TOOLS

Short Answer

1. What is dialogue?

_____

_____

2. What is a memoir?

_____

_____

3. Is Santiago's memoir biographical or autobiographical? What makes it so?

_____

_____

Selection Test 4.9.16

"Something Could Happen to You"

INSIGHTFUL READING

True or False

_____ 1. Santiago and her family came to Brooklyn to get medical help for her brother.

_____ 2. The weather was nice when they arrived in New York.

_____ 3. Santiago's mother always warns her, "Something could happen to you."

_____ 4. Their house in Puerto Rico was less substantial than their house in Brooklyn.

_____ 5. Santiago could sing "The Star Spangled Banner" from beginning to end in English.

Multiple Choice

Circle the letter of the correct answer.

1. How old was the author when she moved to the United States?

   a. five

   b. nine

   c. thirteen

   d. twenty

2. What does the neighbor girl tell Santiago?

   a. that Hispanic and Puerto Rican are the same thing

   b. that her parents are Cuban

   c. that she wants to be her friend

   d. that they will be in the same class

3. Who is Raymond?

   a. Santiago's uncle

   b. Santiago's father

   c. Santiago's neighbor

   d. Santiago's brother

4. Where do Santiago and her siblings stay while her mother works?

   a. with Tata

   b. with a neighbor

   c. in a day-care center

   d. with their mother at work

5. Why is Santiago placed in the class with students with behavioral problems?

   a. because she is a troubled teen

   b. because she had a learning disability

   c. because she could not speak English

   d. because she scored low on an intelligence test

VOCABULARY IN CONTEXT

Sentence Completion

Fill in each blank below with the most appropriate word from Words for Everyday Use from "Something Could Happen to You." You may not use every word, and you may have to change the tense of some words.

gait   ephemeral   pungent   lanky   fastidious   marred   demerit

1. The _____ odor of the onion pervaded the room.

2. The _____ teen was unable to find jeans that fit properly.

3. The _____ man kept an immaculate apartment.

4. She received a(n) _____ for talking during the lecture.

5. His _____ was marked by a characteristic swagger.

UNDERSTANDING LITERARY CONCEPTS

Short Answer

1. What is revealed about Santiago's mother through her dialogue?

   _____

   _____

2. What does Santiago's dialogue as she watches cartoons reveal?

   _____

   _____

3. What aim do you think Santiago had in writing this memoir?

   _____

   _____

CRITICAL WRITING

Essay

Choose <u>one</u> of the following prompts and write an essay. Complete <u>both</u> the Prepare to Write and Write sections of the prompt you choose. Use your own paper as necessary.

1. Ethnic Identity

PREPARE TO WRITE. Consider the fact that Santiago was placed in a class for students with behavioral problems, those who scored low on intelligence tests, and those who planned to drop out when they turned sixteen. She belonged in a more accelerated class, but was denied this opportunity because of her lack of English proficiency. In the space below, list events in the selection that make her feel anxious or inferior.

_____

_____

_____

_____

_____

_____

WRITE. In a brief essay, discuss the ways Santiago learns to regard her ethnic identity. Use evidence from the text to support your analysis.

_____

_____

_____

_____

_____

_____

_____

_____

_____

_____

_____

_____

_____

_____

_____

2. Puerto Rican versus Hispanic

PREPARE TO WRITE. In the space below, write notes on how others identify Santiago as Hispanic instead of Puerto Rican. What effect does this have on her and how she thinks of herself?

_____

_____

_____

_____

_____

_____

_____

_____

_____

_____

WRITE. In a brief essay, analyze the way Santiago as a girl tries to sort out her ethnic identity. In the end, does she perceive herself more as Hispanic or Puerto Rican? Use evidence from the selection to support your response.

_____

_____

_____

_____

_____

_____

_____

_____

_____

_____

_____

_____

_____

_____

_____

_____

_____

Selection Worksheet 9.9

"After You, My Dear Alphonse," page 764

READER RESPONSE ACTIVITIES

Graphic Organizer, page 764

Fill in the chart below listing the assumptions made by Mrs. Wilson about Boyd and the stereotypes about African Americans that she has. One example has been done for you.

Assumptions	Stereotypes
Johnny made Boyd carry the wood	Whites order African Americans around

Reader's Journal, page 764

When have you made an assumption about another person only to discover later that you were wrong?

_____

_____

_____

_____

Guided Reading Questions

PAGE 765

What is Mrs. Wilson baking?

_____

_____

Who is Johnny's friend?

_____

_____

PAGE 766

What game were the boys playing?

_____

_____

What action indicates that Johnny is polite?

_____

_____

What does Mrs. Wilson assume about Boyd?

_____

_____

What job does Boyd's father have?

_____

_____

What does Boyd's sister plan to do?

_____

_____

PAGE 767

What does Mrs. Wilson do when Boyd rejects her offer of clothing?

_____

_____

What does Mrs. Wilson tell Boyd? Why?

_____

_____

Respond to the Selection, page 768

If you were Johnny, what would you say to your mother about what happened at lunch? Would you be angry or happy with how she treated Boyd?

_____

_____

_____

_____

INVESTIGATE, INQUIRE, AND IMAGINE, PAGE 768

Recall

1a. Whom does Johnny invite home for lunch?

_____

_____

_____

2a. What does Mrs. Wilson offer Boyd?

_____

_____

_____

3a. How does Boyd respond to the offer of used clothing?

_____

_____

_____

Analyze

4a. Identify proof that Johnny and Boyd are not aware of Mrs. Wilson's racist attitudes.

_____

_____

_____

Evaluate

5a. Mrs. Wilson tells Boyd, "I'm just disappointed in you." Evaluate the cause of Mrs. Wilson's disappointment.

_____

_____

_____

_____

Interpret

1b. How does Mrs. Wilson's behavior change once she sees Boyd is African American?

_____

_____

_____

2b. What attitude underlies Mrs. Wilson's seemingly generous gestures?

_____

_____

_____

3b. How does Mrs. Wilson feel when Boyd rejects the clothes? How can you tell?

_____

_____

_____

Synthesize

4b. Why doesn't Boyd get angry with Mrs. Wilson?

_____

_____

_____

_____

Extend

5b. What role did Mrs. Wilson want Boyd to play? What roles do you play in your life? How do you decide how to play these roles? Which roles are decided for you?

_____

_____

_____

_____

_____

UNDERSTANDING LITERATURE, PAGE 768

CHARACTER. Is Mrs. Wilson a static or a dynamic character? Why? What character traits does she possess?

_____

_____

_____

_____

_____

STEREOTYPE. Review the chart you completed for the Graphic Organizer. What stereotypes are presented in this short story? How does Boyd defy these stereotypes? What is his experience with stereotypes?

_____

_____

_____

_____

_____

_____

_____

_____

_____

_____

_____

WRITER'S JOURNAL, PAGE 769

1. Imagine that you are Johnny. Write a **journal entry** describing your friend Boyd and explaining why you value his friendship.

_____

_____

_____

_____

_____

_____

_____

_____

2. Imagine that Boyd talks to his mother about Mrs. Wilson's offer of clothes and about the other questions she asked him. Write a **letter** that Boyd's mother mails to Mrs. Wilson.

_____

_____

_____

_____

_____

_____

_____

_____

_____

3. Write a **dialogue** between Mr. and Mrs. Boyd in which Mrs. Boyd describes what transpired at lunch and Mr. Boyd poses questions and makes comments.

_____

_____

_____

_____

_____

_____

_____

_____

_____

_____

_____

INTEGRATING THE LANGUAGE ARTS, PAGE 769

Language, Grammar, and Style

COMPOUND, COMPLEX, AND COMPOUND-COMPLEX SENTENCES. Read about compound, complex, and compound-complex sentences in the Language Arts Survey 3.36, "Combining and Expanding Sentences." Then identify each of the following sentences as a compound sentence, a complex sentence, or a compound-complex sentence.

1. Mrs. Wilson told Johnny to bring in his friend, since Johnny had invited him.

_____

2. The boy didn't know yet what he wanted to be.

_____

3. Boyd's father had given him the wood; therefore, he carried it.

_____

4. After leaving the house, Boyd was relieved.

_____

5. After they have eaten lunch, the boys will be soldiers, and they will play with tanks.

_____

Applied English

AGENDA. Imagine that you belong to an organization called "Youth for Understanding," which has the aim of bringing together the different racial groups in your community. Write an agenda for the organization's first meeting. An agenda outlines things to be considered or done. What is your organization's goal? What groups do you want to bring together? What activities do you want to plan?

_____

_____

_____

_____

_____

_____

_____

_____

_____

_____

_____

_____

_____

_____

_____

_____

_____

_____

_____

_____

_____

Selection Check Test 4.9.17

"After You, My Dear Alphonse"

CHECKING YOUR READING

Short Answer

1. What is the first assumption Mrs. Wilson makes about Boyd?

   _____

2. What does Mrs. Wilson say to Boyd about lunch?

   _____

3. Does she mean what she says? How do you know?

   _____

4. What does Mrs. Wilson's response to Boyd's statement that his sister is going to be a teacher imply?

   _____

5. Why do you think Mrs. Wilson is disappointed in Boyd?

   _____

VOCABULARY IN CONTEXT

Sentence Completion

Fill in each blank below with the most appropriate word from Words for Everyday Use from "After You, My Dear Alphonse." You may not use every word, and you may have to change the tense of some words.

kindling   stewed   foreman   impulse   foxhole

1. My father works as a(n) _____ at a local glass factory.

2. I tried to stave off the _____ to buy the expensive shoes.

3. They were unable to start the fire because they didn't have _____.

LITERARY TOOLS

Matching

Write the letter of the correct answer in the blank provided.

_____ 1. an uncritically accepted, fixed, or conventional idea

_____ 2. a character who changes during the course of action

_____ 3. a character who does not change during the course of action

    a. dynamic character

    b. static character

    c. stereotype

Selection Test 4.9.18

"After You, My Dear Alphonse"

INSIGHTFUL READING

True or False

_____ 1. Mrs. Wilson is African American.

_____ 2. Mrs. Wilson assumes that Jimmy made Boyd carry the wood.

_____ 3. Mrs. Wilson assumes that Boyd's father is a factory worker.

_____ 4. Mrs. Wilson thinks that Boyd's sister will make a good teacher.

_____ 5. Mrs. Wilson assumes that Boyd's family is wealthy.

Short Answer

1. Name three things that Mrs. Wilson assumes about Boyd and his family.

   _____

   _____

2. Is Mrs. Wilson correct in her assumptions?

   _____

   _____

3. What do her assumptions say about her character?

   _____

   _____

4. Do you think Boyd understands why Mrs. Wilson acts the way she does? Explain.

   _____

   _____

5. Do you think Mrs. Wilson realizes that she is prejudiced? Explain.

   _____

   _____

UNDERSTANDING LITERARY CONCEPTS

Identification

Identify each of the following characters as *static* or *dynamic* and write the answer in the blank provided.

_____ 1. Mrs. Wilson

_____ 2. Jimmy

_____ 3. Boyd

Short Answer

1. What stereotypes does Mrs. Wilson hold about African Americans?

_____

_____

2. Which stereotypes of Mrs. Wilson's do Boyd and his family break?

_____

_____

CRITICAL WRITING

Essay

Choose <u>one</u> of the following prompts and write an essay. Complete <u>both</u> the Prepare to Write and Write sections of the prompt you choose. Use your own paper as necessary.

1. Pervading Prejudice

PREPARE TO WRITE. Note that the two boys are pretending that the pieces of wood are "dead Japanese." Also, note that Mrs. Wilson gives no reprimand for this answer. What does this say about the tolerance and acceptance of prejudice? Consider the fact that this story was written shortly after World War II, when Japanese were considered enemies of the United States.

_____

_____

_____

_____

WRITE. In an essay, discuss the implications of the prejudice displayed by the two boys, as well as that of Mrs. Wilson. How might the boys have learned their behavior?

_____

_____

_____

_____

_____

_____

_____

_____

_____

_____

2. Mrs. Wilson's Disappointment

PREPARE TO WRITE. Consider the reasons for Mrs. Wilson's disappointment. Do you think she was disappointed because Boyd did not live up to her stereotype? because she wanted to do something nice and he wouldn't let her? because she wanted to appear to be a charitable person and Boyd denied her that chance?

_____

_____

_____

_____

WRITE. In an essay, state your opinion of why Mrs. Wilson is disappointed with Boyd. Support your opinion with quotations from the text.

_____

_____

_____

_____

_____

_____

_____

_____

_____

_____

_____

_____

_____

Selection Worksheet 9.10

"I Remember; I Believe," page 770

READER RESPONSE ACTIVITIES

Graphic Organizer, page 770

Complete the cluster chart below listing what the speaker does not know.

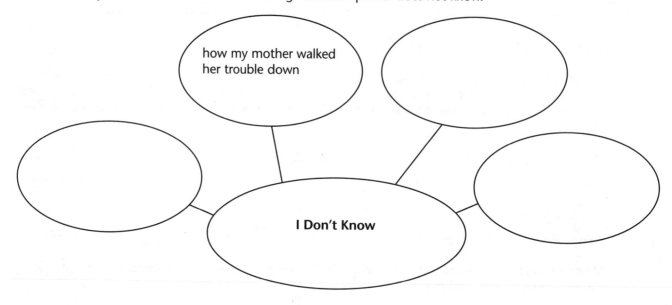

Reader's Journal, page 770

Do you think memories are important? Why, or why not?

_____

_____

_____

_____

Guided Reading Questions

PAGE 771

What doesn't the speaker know about his mother?

_____

_____

What does God do for the speaker?

_____

_____

Art Note, page 771

Autobiography: Water/Ancestors/Middle Passage/Family Ghosts, **1988. Howardena Pindell.**

Howardena Pindell's (1943–   ) painted autobiography includes the central figure of herself immersed in water, her arms moving as if swimming. She is surrounded by pictures of relatives and ancestors, and texts of racist laws of the past. The "middle passage" refers to the route across the ocean taken by slave ships, of which there is a diagram in the lower left. In the context of those elements, what do you think Pindell means by the metaphor of swimming?

_____

_____

_____

_____

Respond to the Selection, page 772

What do you believe you are called to do? Do you believe you are put on this Earth for a specific reason? Why, or why not?

_____

_____

_____

_____

INVESTIGATE, INQUIRE, AND IMAGINE, PAGE 772

Recall

1a. What does the speaker not know about her people?

_____

_____

_____

2a. What does the speaker not know about herself in the third stanza?

_____

_____

_____

3a. In the fourth stanza, what does the speaker say she is going to do?

_____

_____

_____

Interpret

1b. Why is this hard to perceive?

_____

_____

_____

2b. Based on her thoughts in stanza 3, what do you think is her attitude toward life?

_____

_____

_____

3b. What type of person raises his or her voice for justice?

_____

_____

_____

Analyze

4a. For stanzas 1–3, describe the things that the speaker doesn't know.

_____

_____

_____

_____

Synthesize

4b. How is the speaker able to "believe" when she does not know why or how things are the way they are?

_____

_____

_____

_____

Evaluate

5a. Do you think the title is appropriate for this song? Why, or why not?

_____

_____

_____

_____

Extend

5b. For decades after the Holocaust, many Holocaust survivors kept silent for various reasons—to forget or to hide their shame are just two of those reasons. Today, there is a whole genre in literature entitled Holocaust Literature that speaks against this silence. Why do you think oppressed peoples want to remember their past? their history? Why do you think they fight against silence?

_____

_____

_____

_____

_____

Understanding Literature, page 772

Repetition. What does the repetition in this selection indicate about the speaker's focus? What is the speaker dwelling on?

_____

_____

_____

_____

Theme. Review the cluster chart you completed for the Graphic Organizer. What possible themes from this song can you name? What is the speaker saying about memory and remembering the past? How does repetition work toward emphasizing the themes in the song?

_____

_____

_____

_____

WRITER'S JOURNAL, PAGE 773

1. Write a **letter** to Dr. Reagon, describing the effect her song had on you.

_____

_____

_____

_____

_____

_____

_____

_____

_____

_____

_____

_____

_____

_____

_____

_____

2. Write a **memorial** to those people in history (people with which you most identify) who sacrificed and endured hardships fighting for the rights you now have.

_____

_____

_____

_____

_____

_____

_____

_____

_____

_____

_____

_____

_____

_____

3. Pretend you are a high school teacher. Write a **recommendation** to your choir director requesting that the song "I Remember; I Believe" be sung during next year's Black History Month at your school.

_____

_____

_____

_____

_____

_____

_____

_____

_____

_____

_____

_____

_____

_____

_____

_____

_____

_____

INTEGRATING THE LANGUAGE ARTS, PAGE 773

Language, Grammar, and Style

APOSTROPHES. Read the Language Arts Survey 3.90, "Apostrophes." Then circle the correctly punctuated word for each of the following sentences.

1. Dr. Bernice (Reagons', Reagon's) interests are music and history.

2. Sweet Honey in the Rock? (Its', It's) an a cappella ensemble comprised of five African-American women.

3. They (cant', can't) sing without hand percussion instruments.

4. The group (doesn't, does'nt) use anything but traditional music techniques.

5. (That's, Thats') how Reagon fuses her love of music and history—by writing songs that address the African-American experience.

Study and Research

RESEARCHING A HISTORICAL BLACK MOVEMENT OR EVENT. Research a historical black movement or event. What incidents, ideas, and/or attitudes led to the development of the movement or event? Who were the most important figures in the movement? What was the movement or event about? How did it impact or change race relations among Americans? Is our society continuing to feel the effects from the movement or event? If yes, how so? If no, why not? Use the research log below to record your findings and to note the sources you consulted in your research.

Research Log

Research Findings on a Black Movement/Event:

_____

_____

_____

_____

_____

_____

_____

_____

_____

_____

_____

_____

_____

_____

_____

_____

_____

_____

Sources Used:

_____

_____

_____

_____

_____

Selection Check Test 4.9.19

"I Remember; I Believe"

CHECKING YOUR READING

Short Answer

1. What do you think "walked her trouble down" means?

_____

_____

_____

2. What does the universe give the speaker?

_____

_____

_____

3. How are the speaker and her father alike?

_____

_____

_____

LITERARY TOOLS

Short Answer

1. What is repetition?

_____

2. What is a theme?

_____

3. What do themes usually address?

_____

Selection Test 4.9.20

"I Remember; I Believe"

INSIGHTFUL READING

True or False

_____ 1. The speaker does not know how her people survived slavery.

_____ 2. The speaker knows why she is here.

_____ 3. The speaker admires her father.

_____ 4. The speaker believes there is a purpose in her life.

_____ 5. The speaker says the power of the universe does not know her name.

UNDERSTANDING LITERARY CONCEPTS

Short Answer

1. What words and phrases are repeated in the poem?

_____

_____

2. In what way is the structure of the poem repetitious?

_____

_____

3. What do you think is one theme of this poem?

_____

_____

CRITICAL WRITING

Essay

Write an essay, completing <u>both</u> the Prepare to Write and Write sections below. Use your own paper as necessary.

Repetition and Belief

PREPARE TO WRITE. What effect does repetition have on the reader or listener of this poem? Why is the literary technique of repetition especially effective in a poem about the speaker's values and beliefs? Take notes on these questions as you prepare to write your essay.

_____

_____

_____

_____

_____

_____

WRITE. In a brief essay, examine the way the speaker uses repetition to underscore the theme of her poem.

_____

_____

_____

_____

_____

_____

_____

_____

_____

_____

_____

_____

_____

_____

_____

_____

_____

_____

Unit 9 Review/Study Guide

VOCABULARY WORKSHEET

Spelling

Circle the letter of the word that is spelled *incorrectly*. Then write the word correctly on the blank provided.

1. _____
   a. proliferate
   b. tentetive
   c. protocol
   d. genocide

2. _____
   a. aculturation
   b. atrocity
   c. belligerence
   d. intrinsic

3. _____
   a. aesthetic
   b. subdue
   c. comodity
   d. pervade

4. _____
   a. implore
   b. impending
   c. fettered
   d. forman

5. _____
   a. emulate
   b. elite
   c. imemorial
   d. lanky

Synonyms

Circle the letter of the word that comes closest to meaning the *same* as the underlined word.

1. He answered the question with <u>belligerence</u>.

    a. disrespect

    b. combativeness

    c. respect

    d. resolution

2. She exhibits <u>composure</u> in the most stressful moments.

    a. calmness

    b. strength

    c. temper

    d. nervousness

3. The <u>cosmopolitan</u> woman enjoyed the finest clothes.

    a. wealthy

    b. sophisticated

    c. poor

    d. unsophisticated

4. His <u>garish</u> shirt attracted many stares.

    a. tattered

    b. green

    c. gaudy

    d. clean

5. Her mother <u>implored</u> her to stop speeding.

    a. begged

    b. asked

    c. told

    d. commanded

Antonyms

Circle the letter of the word that comes closest to meaning the *opposite* of the underlined word.

1. They made a <u>judicious</u> decision about their budget.

    a. hasty

    b. poor

    c. well informed

    d. sane

2. The memory of her late mother <u>pervaded</u> her thoughts.

   a. consumed

   b. filled

   c. escaped

   d. left

3. The <u>pungent</u> aroma was unbearable.

   a. biting

   b. sharp

   c. mild

   d. sweet

4. She considered the secret <u>sacrosanct</u>.

   a. important

   b. sacred

   c. common knowledge

   d. unimportant

5. The evidence against him was <u>substantial</u>.

   a. important

   b. scarce

   c. unimportant

   d. heavy

Sentence Completion

Fill in each blank below with the most appropriate word from Words for Everyday Use from Unit 9. You may not use every word, and you may have to change the tense of some words.

    aesthetic   demerit   ephemeral   kindling   lank   mesmerized   relegated

1. Santiago and her classmates would receive a(n) _____ if they did not recite the Pledge of Allegiance with zeal.

2. The _____ nature of love is discussed in "Simple Song."

3. Boyd carried _____ into Mrs. Wilson's house.

4. In Álvarez's family, _____ value was placed on skin color.

5. Santiago was _____ by the cartoon.

REVIEW: WORDS FOR EVERYDAY USE

Choose ten words from the list of Words for Everyday Use that you would like to incorporate into your own daily language. For each word, write a short sentence that includes the word in context.

acculturation, 750
aesthetic, 748
aquiline, 747
array, 742
atrocity, 748
belligerence, 749
commodity, 750
composure, 723
concatenation, 731
cosmopolitan, 747
demerit, 760
diaphanous, 750
elite, 748
emulate, 746
entrepreneur, 748
ephemeral, 757
euphemism, 723
fastidious, 760
fettered, 725

foreman, 766
formidable, 723
foxhole, 767
gait, 757
garish, 747
genocide, 748
immemorial, 717
impending, 722
implore, 723
impulse, 766
intrinsic, 750
judicious, 722
kindling, 765
lank, 746
lanky, 759
mackinaw, 741
malapropping, 749
marred, 760
mesmerized, 759

paradigm, 751
patronage, 749
pervade, 725
precarious, 721
proliferate, 750
protocol, 746
pungent, 759
relegated, 748
replenish, 750
sacrosanct, 748
severed, 756
solidarity, 752
stewed, 766
subdue, 760
substantial, 758
subtle, 757
tentative, 731
vacate, 759

1. Word: _____

   Word in context: _____

2. Word: _____

   Word in context: _____

3. Word: _____

   Word in context: _____

4. Word: _____

   Word in context: _____

5. Word: _____

   Word in context: _____

6. Word: _____

   Word in context: _____

7. Word: _____

   Word in context: _____

8. Word: _____

   Word in context: _____

9. Word: _____

   Word in context: _____

10. Word: _____

    Word in context: _____

REVIEW: LITERARY TOOLS

Define each of the following terms, giving concrete examples of how they are used in the selections in this unit. To review a term, refer to the page number indicated or to the Handbook of Literary Terms.

character, 764
characterization, 720, 734
dialogue, 755
first-person point of view, 711
irony, 734
irony of situation, 734
lyric poem, 729

memoir, 755
myth, 715
paradox, 729
personal essay, 745
repetition, 770
sensory details, 740
simile, 715

speaker, 711
stereotype, 764
style, 745
theme, 711, 720, 770
tone, 740, 745

- character _____
  _____

- characterization _____
  _____

- dialogue _____
  _____

- first-person point of view _____
  _____

- irony _____
  _____

- irony of situation _____
  _____

- lyric poem _____
  _____

- memoir _____
  _____

- myth _____
  _____

- paradox _____
  _____

- personal essay _____
  _____

- repetition _____
  _____

• sensory details _____

_____

• simile _____

_____

• speaker _____

_____

• stereotype _____

_____

• style _____

_____

• theme _____

_____

• tone _____

_____

REFLECTING ON YOUR READING

Genre Studies

1. **LYRIC POEM.** A lyric poem is a highly musical verse that expresses the emotions of a speaker. Select a lyric poem from this unit that you like and describe what emotions the speaker is expressing. What examples of language use illustrate these emotions the best?

_____

_____

_____

_____

2. **NONFICTION.** Both "A White Woman of Color" and "Something Could Happen to You" explore the cultural identity of a Hispanic woman. How would you describe the approach each author takes toward expressing her experience? For example, is it narrative, reflective, or analytical? Which do you find the most effective? Why?

_____

_____

_____

_____

3. **SHORT STORY.** In "The Cabuliwallah," Tagore chose the first-person point of view. In "After You, My Dear Alphonse," Jackson chose the third-person point of view. What makes these points of view appropriate for the stories they relate?

_____

_____

_____

_____

Thematic Studies

4. **THE IMMIGRANT EXPERIENCE.** In "The Cabuliwallah," "A White Woman of Color," and "Something Could Happen to You," the fruit peddlar, Álvarez, and Santiago all confront life in a new land. What challenges do they face? What do they have to give up? Who adjusts the best? Why? Who has the most difficulty adjusting? Why? In what way are their lives richer than those of people who have never immigrated? What can we learn from their experiences?

_____

_____

_____

_____

5. **VIOLENCE.** How is violence central to "The Cabuliwallah" and "The Legend"? Was the violence justified? Do the authors take a position for or against violence? What do they say is the price of violence?

_____

_____

_____

_____

6. **DISCRIMINATION.** Who is discriminated against in "The Cabuliwallah" and "After You, My Dear Alphonse"? What is the basis for this discrimination—race, religion, nationality? Who does the discriminating? Are the perpetrators of the discrimination aware of their discrimination? How can you tell?

_____

_____

_____

_____

7. **FRIENDSHIP.** Which stanza of Marge Piercy's poem "Simple Song" reflects the status of the relationship between Mini and Rahmun at the beginning of "The Cabuliwallah"? Which stanza of Piercy's poem reflects the status of the relationship between Mini and Rahmun at the end of the story? What factors account for their separation and distance at the end of the story?

_____

_____

_____

_____

QUESTIONS FOR WRITING, DISCUSSION, AND RESEARCH

1. Review the definition of *stereotype* in the Handbook of Literary Terms. Discuss how stereotypes come into being and the negative effects stereotypes often have. Present several ways that stereotyping can be overcome.

   _____

   _____

   _____

   _____

   _____

   _____

2. Diversity, in ideas and cultures, can add interest and knowledge to a person's life. Discuss the diversity in your school or community, and suggest ways to celebrate that diversity together as a group.

   _____

   _____

   _____

   _____

   _____

   _____

3. Choose one of the authors in this unit to research. Write a report on him or her, focusing on the aspects that make the author's life outstanding or different.

   _____

   _____

   _____

   _____

   _____

   _____

FOR YOUR READING LIST

Independent Reading Activity

A TRIP AROUND THE GLOBE. Choose one culture, connected to people close to you, and do some background research. Report on the heritage of your relatives or other members of your community. Include the background information from your research and information you have gotten from speaking with your family or neighbors.

_____

_____

_____

_____

_____

_____

_____

_____

_____

_____

Unit 9 Test

INSIGHTFUL READING

Matching

Write the letter of the correct answer in the blank provided.

_____ 1. was born in the Dominican Republic and moved to the United States

_____ 2. was accused of stealing by Upton

_____ 3. was befriended by the Cabuliwallah

_____ 4. wanted a new dog

_____ 5. was born in Puerto Rico and moved to the United States

      a. Mini

      b. Wally

      c. Doña Luz

      d. Julia Álvarez

      e. Esmeralda Santiago

True or False

_____ 1. In "The Legend," the victim is shot by a young boy.

_____ 2. In "I Remember; I Believe," the speaker does not understand why she is still here.

_____ 3. In "After You, My Dear Alphonse," Mrs. Wilson gives Boyd clothes.

_____ 4. In "Simple Song," the speaker says love cannot outlast the need for newness.

_____ 5. The Cabuliwallah is taken to prison for fraud.

Sentence Completion

Fill in each blank below with the most appropriate word from Words for Everyday Use from Unit 9. You may not use every term, and you may have to change the tense of some words.

     emulate   entrepreneur   fastidious   impulse   mackinaw   marred   subtle

1. The two car models only had _____ differences.

2. The _____ started his own business.

3. He curbed his _____ to have a snack.

4. He wore a(n) ——————————— over his old sweater.

5. She is ——————————— about her work.

UNDERSTANDING LITERARY CONCEPTS

Sentence Completion

Fill in the blanks using the following terms.

character   dialogue   irony   paradox   repetition

1. The accusation of Doña Luz is an example of ———————————.

2. A(n) ——————————— is a person who figures in the action of a literary work.

3. Shirley Jackson uses ——————————— to reveal character.

4. "I Remember; I Believe" contains ———————————.

5. A(n) ——————————— is a seemingly contradictory statement, idea, or event.

CRITICAL WRITING

Short Answer

1. Why do you think the speaker of "Prayer to the Pacific" takes four stones home?

_____

_____

2. Why do you think Wally wants a new dog and other animals?

_____

_____

3. What does the speaker of "I Remember; I Believe" remember?

_____

_____

4. How does Mrs. Wilson's prejudice manifest?

_____

_____

5. How has Mini changed from the time the Cabuliwallah was imprisoned to her wedding day?

_____

_____

Essay

Choose <u>one</u> of the following prompts and write an essay. Complete <u>both</u> the Prepare to Write and Write sections of the prompt you choose. Use your own paper as necessary.

1. Perspective

PREPARE TO WRITE. Both Álvarez and Santiago chronicle their experiences of immigrating to the United States. Consider the ways their perspectives are similar and the ways they differ.

_____

_____

_____

_____

WRITE. In an essay, compare and contrast the events and perspectives in Álvarez's and Santiago's works. Be sure to include support from the texts.

_____

_____

_____

_____

_____

_____

_____

_____

_____

_____

_____

_____

_____

_____

_____

_____

_____

_____

_____

2. Characterization

PREPARE TO WRITE. Choose two stories or poems containing characters from this unit. Then, note which techniques each author uses for characterization. You might make a chart with three columns titled *Description, Portrayal of Behavior,* and *Portrayal of Internal States.*

Description	Portrayal of Behavior	Portrayal of Internal States

WRITE. In an essay, compare and contrast the characterization techniques two authors use. Discuss which characterization you think is most effective. Support your opinions with quotations from the text.

_____

_____

_____

_____

_____

_____

_____

_____

_____

_____

_____

_____

_____

Answer Key

Answer Key

(See the Annotated Teacher's Edition for answers to specific Selection Worksheet activities. Answers to some Vocabulary exercises are provided in this Answer Key.)

SELECTION CHECK TEST 4.9.1

"Simple Song"

CHECKING YOUR READING

Short Answer

1. Piercy possibly means when we fall in love.
2. We perceive the person as like us and easy to spend time with.
3. We perceive the person as hard to talk to, hard to be around, and opposite of us.
4. According to the last stanza, neither of those perceptions is exactly correct.
5. Students may say that the lines mean that love is not as strong as our need for newness and excitement.

LITERARY TOOLS

Matching

1. d. theme
2. a. speaker
3. c. third-person point of view
4. b. first-person point of view

SELECTION TEST 4.9.2

"Simple Song"

INSIGHTFUL READING

True or False

1. True
2. False
3. True
4. False
5. True

UNDERSTANDING LITERARY CONCEPTS

Short Answer

1. The poem is presented from the first-person point of view, which is evident from the speaker's use of *we*.
2. Students may say that the use of first-person point of view allows the speaker to address the reader and include him or her in the *we*.
3. She builds up to this theme by contrasting new love to separation. Then she explains the reason for the separation.

CRITICAL WRITING

Essay

Students should write an essay based on <u>one</u> of the prompts.

1. Stanzas

Responses will vary, but students should note that the first stanza examines the way a person feels when a relationship begins; the second stanza examines the way a person feels when a relationship ends; and the third stanza comments on these two feelings.

2. Do You Agree?

Responses will vary, but students might note that the author tries to make the poem universal by including the pronouns *we* and *you*.

SELECTION CHECK TEST 4.9.3

"Prayer to the Pacific"

CHECKING YOUR READING

Short Answer

1. The speaker travels to the ocean.
2. She returns turquoise and red coral.
3. They symbolize the ocean.
4. They describe the sunset over the Pacific Ocean.

LITERARY TOOLS

Short Answer

1. A simile is a comparison using *like* or *as*.
2. A myth is a story that explains objects or events in the natural world as resulting from the action of some supernatural force or entity.
3. She mentions the myth of origin.

SELECTION TEST 4.9.4

"Prayer to the Pacific"

INSIGHTFUL READING

True or False

1. False
2. True
3. False

Short Answer

1. She describes it as a "southwest land of sandrock."
2. She is visiting the Pacific Ocean. It is evident that the ocean is the Pacific because she watches the sun set over it.

UNDERSTANDING LITERARY CONCEPTS

Short Answer

1. The simile implies that the myth of origin is all-encompassing like the ocean.
2. The migration of Indians from China and the reason rain clouds drift from west to east are both explained by the myth.
3. Yes, Grandfather Turtle is presented.

CRITICAL WRITING

Essay

Students should write an essay based on <u>one</u> of the prompts.

1. Analyzing Literary Techniques in the Poem

Responses will vary, but students might say that Silko personifies the ocean, which she says "sends" turquoise and red coral, like gifts from one person to another. Students may point out various images that they find especially vivid, and they might also note that Silko uses a broad range of senses when describing these images: "Pale / pale water in the yellow-white light of / sun," "Four round stones in my pocket I carry back the ocean / to suck and taste," "Green leaves in the wind / wet earth on my feet / swallowing raindrops / clear from China." Silko uses simile to compare the size of the ocean to the largeness of the "myth of origin." This simile introduces the myth that appears later in the poem. Finally, students might note that a concrete poem is one written in a shape that suggests its subject matter. By breaking the lines of this poem as she does, Silko makes this poem look like ocean waves rolling onto shore.

2. Exploring Myth

Students should note that in this poem Silko tells the myth that thirty thousand years ago, "Indians came riding across the ocean / carried by giant sea turtles." In Silko's telling, the waves were high that day, and the great turtles waded slowly out from the sea; Grandfather turtle rolled in the sand four times before disappearing back into the ocean, "swimming into the sun." Responses will vary as students speculate about the importance of turtles in native myths. They might note that sea turtles are powerful and travel fast in the ocean, and would be thus capable of carrying people on their backs. They also live long lives and are one of the longest-surviving species, thus leading to the belief that they would be connected to the creation of the world.

SELECTION WORKSHEET 9.3

"The Cabuliwallah"

INTEGRATING THE LANGUAGE ARTS

Vocabulary

USING CONTEXT CLUES TO ESTIMATE WORD MEANING
1. impending: about to happen
2. composure: calm appearance; not showing emotion
3. euphemism: term that makes something sound good or inoffensive
4. formidable: strong presence
5. implore: beg, plead

SELECTION CHECK TEST 4.9.5

"The Cabuliwallah"

CHECKING YOUR READING

Short Answer
1. She is five years old.
2. First, she calls him to the house. Then she reacts with fear.
3. They become good friends, constantly talking and joking.
4. He is arrested and taken to jail because he struck one of his customers who refused to pay for goods.
5. She is shy and seems fearful, as she was during their first meeting.

VOCABULARY IN CONTEXT

Sentence Completion

1. formidable
2. impending
3. judicious
4. composure
5. pervaded

LITERARY TOOLS

Short Answer

1. A theme is a central idea in a literary work.
2. Characterization is the use of literary techniques to create a character.
3. Direct description, portrayal of characters' behavior, and representation of characters' internal states are the three major techniques of characterization.

SELECTION TEST 4.9.6

"The Cabuliwallah"

INSIGHTFUL READING

True or False

1. True
2. False
3. True
4. True
5. False

Matching

1. e. Pratap Singh
2. a. Mini
3. d. Cabuliwallah
4. c. Mini's mother
5. b. Mini's father

VOCABULARY IN CONTEXT

Sentence Completion

1. euphemism
2. implored
3. precarious
4. fettered
5. composure

UNDERSTANDING LITERARY TECHNIQUES

Short Answer

1. Students might say one theme deals with the effects of the passage of time; another deals with a girl's coming of age.
2. Students should note that his character is primarily revealed through the representations of his internal states. Tagore also uses the portrayal of the narrator's behavior to reveal character.
3. Tagore does not represent the internal states of these characters.

Essay

Father-Daughter Relationships
Responses will vary, but students might note that the father-daughter relationship is typical in that the two were close when Mini was younger and grew apart as she grew older.

SELECTION CHECK TEST 4.9.7

"New Dog"

CHECKING YOUR READING

Short Answer

1. He has a neurological illness that causes paralysis.
2. He goes to pick up the dog they can't keep.
3. They say they cannot give up their dog.
4. He goes to an animal shelter "just to look."
5. He finds Beau, the "perfect" dog for Wally.

LITERARY TOOLS

Short Answer

1. A paradox is a seemingly contradictory statement, idea, or event.
2. A lyric poem is a highly musical verse that expresses the emotions of a speaker.
3. The speaker expresses confusion over Wally's want of a new attachment and wonder over Wally's ability to pet Beau.

SELECTION TEST 4.9.8

"New Dog"

INSIGHTFUL READING

True or False

1. False
2. True
3. False
4. False
5. True

UNDERSTANDING LITERARY CONCEPTS

Short Answer

1. Students may say that Wally, so ill and unable to move, wanting a dog so full of life is paradoxical.
2. He expresses his emotions by describing events in vivid, emotional detail.
3. Students may say that seeing Wally pet Beau affects the speaker the most.

CRITICAL WRITING

Essay

Students should write an essay based on <u>one</u> of the prompts.

1. Beau's Effect
Responses will vary, but students should note that Beau has provided a new sense of life and energy to Wally's and the speaker's lives.

2. Through Wally's Eyes
Responses will vary.

"1910"

CHECKING YOUR READING

Short Answer

1. She is a strong woman who is not easily affected by events that surround her.
2. She laughs at her terror.
3. Her lips quiver when Upton accuses her of being a thief.
4. Students may say they symbolize the dignity of Doña Luz or that they symbolize her protection from the events that surround her.
5. It burns down.

LITERARY TOOLS

Matching

1. b. irony
2. a. characterization
3. c. irony of situation

SELECTION TEST 4.9.10

"1910"

INSIGHTFUL READING

True or False

1. True
2. True
3. False
4. True
5. False

UNDERSTANDING LITERARY CONCEPTS

Short Answer

1. She is a strong, proud woman.
2. Mora uses direct description and portrayal of behavior to characterize Doña Luz. Mora describes her clothing, "her black shawl, black gloves," and her actions, "her back straight, chin high."
3. It is ironic because she is an upper-class citizen whose presence demands respect in Mexico; but in the United States she is treated as a common criminal.

CRITICAL WRITING

Essay

Students should write an essay based on <u>one</u> of the prompts.

1. Connecting Two Poems

Students should write a comparison-and-contrast essay about the situations in the two poems. In "1910," there is much unrest in both Mexico and the United States (with references to Pancho Villa and Upton's Five-and-Dime burning down). Mexicans are called thieves and a storekeeper makes Doña Luz remove her white gloves and shawl so she cannot steal. In "Not Knowing, in Aztlán," the person addressed as "you" is looked at distrustfully by many different people—schoolteachers, City Hall clerks, cops, and airport marshalls. Both poems deal with the discrimination of someone of a different ethnic background. Both poems regard the main character sympathetically. Students may say that Doña Luz is in a more powerful position, since she does not act helpless or fearful at any point in the poem. The only indication of her fear is when her lips quiver. In the end, Upton's Five-and-Dime has burned to the ground, and Doña Luz is walking over the burned structure with "chin high, / never watching her feet."

2. Character Analysis
Responses will vary, but students should note that Doña Luz is a proud, strong woman. The details that support this include the following: She is the mother of a judge; others bow their heads when she passes; she is called the respectful name of Doña Luz; she always wears a black shawl and white gloves; she carries herself with dignity ("barely toucing her son's wrist / with her fingertips"); she keeps her "back straight, chin high," and never watches her feet.

SELECTION CHECK TEST 4.9.11

"The Legend"

CHECKING YOUR READING

Short Answer
1. The poem is set in Chicago outside of a laundromat during the winter.
2. He has just finished doing his wash for the week.
3. He is a thin Asian man who is dressed in rumpled pants and a dingy coat.
4. He is shot by a boy.
5. The speaker feels ashamed because he feels so distinctly separate from the wounded man.

SELECTION TEST 4.9.12

"The Legend"

INSIGHTFUL READING

True or False
1. False
2. True
3. True
4. False
5. False

UNDERSTANDING LITERARY CONCEPTS

Short Answer
1. The quotation appeals to sight.
2. Students might say a serious tone of disbelief.
3. Students might say the tone is one of caring and well-wishing.

CRITICAL WRITING

Essay

Students should write an essay based on <u>one</u> of the prompts.

1. Analyzing Images of Light
The man finishes his laundry and "steps into the twilight of early evening." The quality of light is then described as a "Rembrandt glow on his face, / a triangle of orange in the hollow of his cheek, / as a last flash of sunset / blazes the storefronts and lit windows of the street." As the man dies, Hongo says, "Let the night sky cover him." Students might note that the shift from light to darkness connects to the man's passage from life to death. His final action is the completed laundry, after which he is illuminated with the Rembrandt glow and the sunset flashes around him. As he dies, the night covers him in darkness.

2. The Speaker
Responses will vary, but students might say that the speaker cares more than he realizes. He remarks that he is ashamed for feeling so separate, but he acknowledges the distinction and recalls the emotional aspects of the incident in detail.

"A White Woman of Color"

INTEGRATING THE LANGUAGE ARTS

Vocabulary

USING BASE WORDS. Responses will vary, depending on the dictionary used. Sample responses are given.

1. dia<u>phan</u>ous
   Greek; characterized by such fineness of texture as to permit seeing through
2. aes<u>thet</u>ic or <u>aesthet</u>ic
   Greek; of, relating to, or dealing with the beautiful
3. <u>gar</u>ish
   etymology unknown; excessively vivid; flashy
4. <u>gen</u>ocide or <u>gen</u>ocide
   Greek; deliberate and systematic destruction of a racial, political, or cultural group
5. para<u>digm</u>
   Greek; philosophical or theoretical framework consisting of theories and generalizations
6. <u>patron</u>age
   Latin; support or influence of a patron; kindness done with an air of superiority
7. proto<u>col</u>
   Greek; code entailing strict adherence to etiquette
8. rele<u>gat</u>ed or rele<u>gat</u>ed
   Latin; assigned to a place of insignificance or oblivion
9. re<u>plen</u>ish
   Latin; fill or build up again
10. <u>solidar</u>ity
    Latin; unity based on community interests, objectives, and standards

---

SELECTION CHECK TEST 4.9.13

"A White Woman of Color"

CHECKING YOUR READING

Short Answer

1. She experiences racism.
2. The racism manifests in the hierarchy of beauty—the lighter the skin and the straighter the hair, the more beautiful a girl was considered.
3. She was a white woman, both in terms of race and class. She was proper and considered part of the elite class.
4. He was dark-skinned with coarse hair. He came from a country family of twenty-five children. His family was educated, but only in the Dominican Republic.
5. She has learned to fear the word *exclusive* because it breeds racism and hatred.

VOCABULARY IN CONTEXT

Sentence Completion

1. protocol
2. elite
3. emulate
4. replenish
5. relegated

Matching

1. b. tone
2. c. personal essay
3. a. style

SELECTION TEST 4.9.14

"A White Woman of Color"

INSIGHTFUL READING

True or False

1. True
2. False
3. True
4. False
5. True

Multiple Choice

1. d. considered the least beautiful because of her coarse features
2. a. did not reside exclusively among the whites
3. b. everyone's family had dark members
4. c. "Jamaica Estates"
5. a. OTHER

VOCABULARY IN CONTEXT

Sentence Completion

1. cosmopolitan
2. garish
3. atrocity
4. aquiline
5. commodity

UNDERSTANDING LITERARY CONCEPTS

Short Answer

1. Students may say that her aim was to inform, to persuade, or to share her personal experience.
2. Students may say that this essay has a serious tone.
3. Students might consider the style informal and familiar.

CRITICAL WRITING

Essay

Students should write an essay based on <u>one</u> of the prompts.

1. Redefining Ethnicity
Responses will vary, but students should be able to restate Álvarez's words to show that she realizes that a person cannot be assumed to be a certain way simply because of his or her ethnic background. Álvarez gives many examples throughout her essay that support this statement. They include insights from her own family: many of Papi's siblings were college educated, even though some people might expect they would not be, being from the country and being of a dark color. The hierarchy of beauty in her own family was determined by skin color; a person's manners and habits were also scrutinized with assumptions based on these observations. Beyond these family observations, Álvarez discovered that race was an even greater issue once the family moved to America. The family was light-skinned enough to live in Jamaica Estates, while an African-American family had greater struggles there. She and her sisters were taunted for where they were from nevertheless. When Álvarez began college, multiculturalism was being celebrated, and she found her ethnic background being treated like a commodity.

2. The Multicultural, Multiracial Model

Responses will vary, but students should discuss the ethnic divisions that Álvarez encountered (see the answer to the first prompt, above). They should also evaluate whether Latinos can provide a positive multicultural, multiracial model to America. They may want to discuss the way Álvarez herself shows the way different ethnic boundaries have overlapped and have been erased in her own life. As a Dominican, she points out that she cannot compartmentalize herself on questionnaires as being of one race; she is also uncertain whether the category of "Hispanic" really reflects who she is. The title of this essay, "A White Woman of Color," also reflects this paradox. At the same time, Álvarez clearly accepts and celebrates the richness in her multicultural identity, and in that way presents an example of a positive role model.

SELECTION WORKSHEET 9.8

"Something Could Happen to You"

INTEGRATING THE LANGUAGE ARTS

Vocabulary

USING SUFFIXES

1. b. scrupulous
2. i. tall
3. j. make free
4. e. acrid
5. f. cut
6. d. fascinated
7. g. temporary
8. a. damaged
9. c. sturdy
10. h. native of Cuba

SELECTION CHECK TEST 4.9.15

"Something Could Happen to You"

CHECKING YOUR READING

Short Answer

1. It was hot, humid, and stormy.
2. She thought New York was darker and dirtier than she expected.
3. She tells Santiago that *Hispanic* and *Puerto Rican* are the same thing.
4. She feels as if she is someone else, and knowing that made her fear the dangers that lay ahead.
5. She is placed in the class because she spoke no English.

VOCABULARY IN CONTEXT

Sentence Completion

1. subtle
2. vacate
3. mesmerized
4. severed
5. subdued

Short Answer

1. Dialogue is conversation involving two or more characters.
2. A memoir is a nonfiction narration that tells a story.
3. Her memoir is autobiographical.

SELECTION TEST 4.9.16

"Something Could Happen to You"

INSIGHTFUL READING

True or False

1. True
2. False
3. True
4. False
5. True

Multiple Choice

1. c. thirteen
2. a. that Hispanic and Puerto Rican are the same thing
3. d. Álvarez's brother
4. a. with Tata
5. c. because she could not speak English

VOCABULARY IN CONTEXT

Sentence Completion

1. pungent
2. lanky
3. fastidious
4. demerit
5. gait

UNDERSTANDING LITERARY CONCEPTS

Short Answer

1. Her main dialogue, "Something could happen to you," reveals her fear of the city and her concern for her daughter.
2. This dialogue reveals her lack of English proficiency.
3. Students may say that she wanted to tell a story or to make a point.

CRITICAL WRITING

Essay

Students should write an essay based on <u>one</u> of the prompts.

1. Ethnic Identity

Responses will vary, but students should include examples of Santiago's uneasiness or nervousness in being placed in the class with struggling learners. She writes of her hands shaking, of the "unfamiliar waves of sound" cresting over her head, and how she wants to "float up and out of that classroom, away from the hostile air that filled every corner of it, every crevice." The narrator wants to disappear. Santiago provides a translation of "The Star Spangled Banner," showing exactly how confusing the new language was for her. She also recounts how everyone was required to recite the Pledge of Allegiance perfectly, even though they did not understand the words. As humorous as some of these events might be, they point to an ongoing source of feeling inferior.

2. Puerto Rican versus Hispanic

For Santiago, the question of whether she is Puerto Rican or Hispanic begins when a girl in the neighborhood says she is Hispanic if she speaks Spanish. The girl first says that being Puerto Rican equals being Hispanic, but then says that "your parents have to be Puerto Rican or Cuban or something." After the girls discuss whether a person can be Hispanic without speaking Spanish, Santiago concludes, "I'd always been Puerto Rican, and it hadn't occurred to me that in Brooklyn I'd be someone else." Students may find that Santiago does not ultimately decide whether she is more Hispanic or Puerto Rican. She is simply trying to sort out who she is and trying to survive and assimilate into her new environment.

SELECTION CHECK TEST 4.9.17

"After You, My Dear Alphonse"

CHECKING YOUR READING

Short Answer

1. She assumes that Boyd was forced to carry the wood.
2. She says that there is plenty of food and that he can have all he wants.
3. She obviously does not mean it because she takes away the gingerbread as Boyd is reaching for another piece.
4. Her response implies that she believes his sister will not actually be able to teach. She is condescending to him by patting him on the head.
5. Students may say that she is disappointed because he and his family have not lived up to the stereotype she has set in her mind.

VOCABULARY IN CONTEXT

Sentence Completion

1. foreman
2. impulse
3. kindling

LITERARY TOOLS

Matching

1. c. stereotype
2. a. dynamic character
3. b. static character

SELECTION TEST 4.9.18

"After You, My Dear Alphonse"

INSIGHTFUL READING

True or False

1. False
2. True
3. True
4. False
5. False

Short Answer

1. Students may name the following assumptions: that Boyd's father works in a factory; that his mother works; and that his sister will never become a teacher.
2. No, she is not entirely correct. She assumes that his father is a laborer, when in actuality he is a foreman. She assumes that his mother works because they need the money, but she does not work. We do not know whether his sister becomes a teacher, but it is likely that she does.
3. The assumptions she makes reflect her stereotypical and prejudiced perception of African Americans.
4. Students may say that Boyd doesn't seem to understand because of his simple responses and his worry that Mrs. Wilson may still be angry with him.
5. Students should note that she does not see herself as prejudiced. She sees herself as a charitable woman and Boyd as an ungrateful child.

UNDERSTANDING LITERARY CONCEPTS

Identification

1. static
2. static
3. static

Short Answer

1. She holds the stereotypes that African Americans are all laborers, that both parents must work, that white people order them around, that they have no chance of holding white-collar jobs, and that they are poor.
2. They break all of the stereotypes that she holds.

CRITICAL WRITING

Essay

Students should write an essay based on <u>one</u> of the prompts.

1. Pervading Prejudice
Responses will vary, but students might suggest that the boys learned their behavior from the media and from their families.

2. Mrs. Wilson's Disappointment
Responses will vary, but students are likely to say that Mrs. Wilson is disappointed because Boyd did not live up to her stereotype.

SELECTION CHECK TEST 4.9.19

"I Remember; I Believe"

CHECKING YOUR READING

Short Answer

1. Students may say that it means "dealt with her trouble" or "did not let the trouble bother her."
2. It gives her a song to sing.
3. He "stands his ground" and she raises her "voice for justice." Both fight for their rights.

LITERARY TOOLS

Short Answer

1. Repetition is the writer's conscious reuse of a sound, word, phrase, sentence, or other element.
2. A theme is a central idea in a literary work.
3. Themes usually address universal topics, such as love, death, family, and friendship.

"I Remember; I Believe"

INSIGHTFUL READING

True or False

1. True
2. False
3. True
4. True
5. False

UNDERSTANDING LITERARY CONCEPTS

Short Answer

1. Students should note the following: *I don't know how; I don't know why; I believe.*
2. She begins every line but one with the word *I*. Her sentences are parallel, as are her stanzas.
3. Students may say one theme is that despite hardships, one must continue to live and fight for justice.

CRITICAL WRITING

Essay

Repetition and Belief

Responses will vary, but students may note that the speaker repeats the phrases "I don't know" and "I believe" to emphasize the way she can have faith in things she does not understand intellectually. For example, the speaker does not know how people can endure injustice, yet she believes such endurance is possible because history witnesses that her people have survived slavery. She doesn't know how she "rates" to start another day, yet because she is still alive, she believes. Students may find that the technique of repetition in this poem helps reinforce the speaker's beliefs. They may also note that many poems of faith as well as prayers use repetition to emphasize statements of belief.

Vocabulary Worksheet

Spelling

1. b. tentative
2. a. acculturation
3. c. commodity
4. d. foreman
5. c. immemorial

Synonyms

1. b. combativeness
2. a. calmness
3. b. sophisticated
4. c. gaudy
5. a. begged

Antonyms

1. a. hasty
2. d. left
3. c. mild
4. d. unimportant
5. b. scarce

Sentence Completion

1. demerit
2. ephemeral
3. kindling
4. aesthetic
5. mesmerized

Review: Words for Everyday Use
Responses will vary.

Review: Literary Tools
Responses will vary.

Reflecting on Your Reading

Genre Studies

Responses will vary.

Thematic Studies

Responses will vary.

Questions for Writing, Discussion, and Research

1. Responses will vary, but students might note that stereotypes often lead to misjudgments and unfair treatment because of a false belief.
2. Responses will vary.
3. Responses will vary.

For Your Reading List

Independent Reading Activity

A Trip around the Globe. Responses will vary.

INSIGHTFUL READING

Matching

1. d. Julia Álvarez
2. c. Doña Luz
3. a. Mini
4. b. Wally
5. e. Esmeralda Santiago

True or False

1. True
2. False
3. False
4. True
5. False

Sentence Completion

1. subtle
2. entrepreneur
3. impulse
4. mackinaw
5. fastidious

UNDERSTANDING LITERARY CONCEPTS

Sentence Completion

1. irony
2. character
3. dialogue
4. repetition
5. paradox

CRITICAL WRITING

Short Answer

1. Students may say she takes the stones home because they will remind her of the ocean, which, in turn, reminds her of the myth of origin.
2. Students may say that he wants to be reminded of activity and of the joy of life.
3. She remembers her mother coping with trouble, her father standing his ground, and the slavery of her people.
4. It manifests in her assumptions and stereotypical beliefs about African Americans. It also manifests in her want to be seen as a charitable person.
5. She has grown up and has reverted back to her bashful self of their first meeting.

Essay

Students should write an essay based on <u>one</u> of the prompts.

1. Perspective

Responses will vary, but students might note that the perspective of Álvarez is one of an adult, whereas Santiago's is from an adolescent point of view.

2. Characterization

Responses will vary.